American Aces of World War 1

SERIES EDITOR: TONY HOLMES

OSPREY AIRCRAFT OF THE ACES® • 42

American Aces of World War 1

Norman Franks

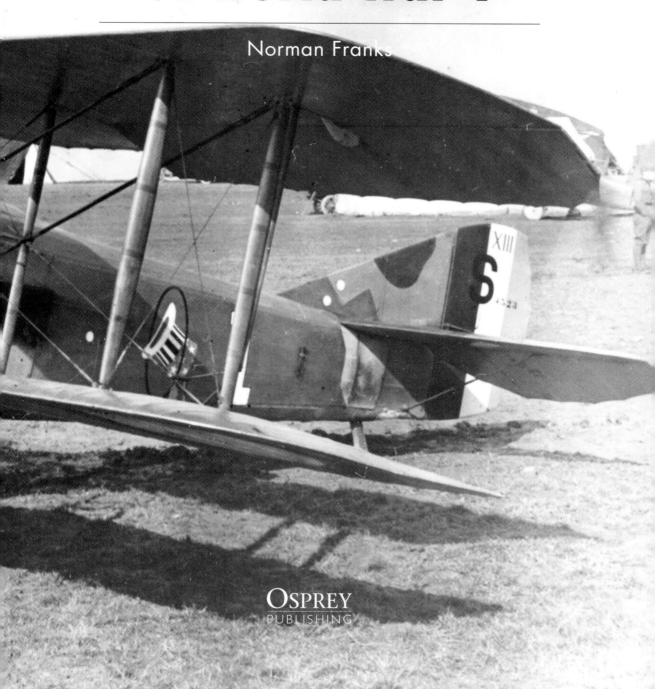

OSPREY
PUBLISHING

Front cover
The SPAD XIII flown by 1st Lt Frank Luke Jr, 27th Aero Squadron, September 1918. Luke scored an amazing 18 victories between 12 and 29 September before being brought down on the wrong side of the lines. In trying to attract attention with his side-arm he was shot and killed by German soldiers

First published in Great Britain in 2001 by Osprey Publishing
Elms Court, Chapel Way, Botley, Oxford, OX2 9LP
Email: info@ospreypublishing.com

ISBN 1 85532 961 1

Page design by TT Designs, T & B Truscott
Cover Artwork by Keith Woodcock
Aircraft Profiles by Harry Dempsey
Scale Drawings by Mark Styling

Origination by Grasmere Digital Imaging, Leeds, UK
Printed in Hong Kong through Bookbuilders

00 01 02 03 04   10 9 8 7 6 5 4 3 2 1

For a catalogue of all Osprey Publishing titles please contact us at:

Osprey Direct UK, PO Box 140, Wellingborough, Northants NN8 4ZA, UK
E-mail: info@ospreydirect.co.uk

Osprey Direct USA, c/o Motorbooks International, 729 Prospect Ave, PO Box 1, Osceola, WI 54020, USA
E-mail: info@ospreydirectusa.com

Or visit our website: www.ospreypublishing.com

CONTENTS

WAR AND ADVENTURE

When World War 1 began in August 1914 and Germany invaded France and Belgium, it all seemed very far away from the United States of America. The American government stayed neutral until finally entering the war on 6 April 1917, the last of the major Allied Powers to do so. Nevertheless there were some Americans who felt it their duty to head for France to volunteer their help in the Allied cause. For the most part, those volunteering did so with the American Ambulance Service, a peaceful and humanitarian way of helping the French.

In 1914–15, few Americans had seen an aeroplane while others had only heard of such things in far off Europe. There can be little doubt that those men who went off to help France in the first months of the war had

Elliott White Springs epitomises the spirit of the young American 'knights of the air'. Having trained as an aviation cadet he became a 16-victory ace with No 85 Squadron RAF and the 148th Aero (see Chapter 5). After the war he wrote a number of best-selling aviation books, became a multi-millionaire businessman and served in the US Army Air Corps in World War 2 *(Bruce Robertson)*

no dreams of taking to the skies in the frail craft of the day. As long as the USA stayed neutral, the only way American nationals could fight for France was to join the French Foreign Legion, or to join the British Royal Flying Corps in Canada, often giving their nationality as Canadian.

As the war developed, Americans who did see aviation service can be said to fall into three main categories: those who enlisted in the French Aviation Service, those who travelled to Canada in order to join the Royal Flying Corps (RFC) or Royal Naval Air Service (RNAS) – which amalgamated in 1918 to form the Royal Air Force (RAF) – and those who enlisted directly in the US Air Service (USAS). Once America came into the war, the majority joined directly into the US Air Service, which, once in France, came under the French system of doing things, and, initially under French jurisdiction.

The Americans also adopted the French system of counting victory scores, which were generally very strict over confirmation of hostile aircraft destroyed, but like the French – and the British – could share kills among a group of pilots if each had taken part. This was very different from the German system where only one pilot was credited with a victory, sometimes the toss of a coin deciding who would be able to add a kill to his score.

While the destruction of hostile aeroplanes was important, it was just as important for the fighter pilots to wrestle air supremacy over the battle fronts, in order for the two-seater reconnaissance and bombing machines to do their jobs as unrestricted as possible. Thus the vast majority of pilots, whilst never reaching the dizzy heights of 'ace', flew, fought and successfully 'did the job'.

Pilots of No 32 Squadron study a map on the fuselage of an S.E.5a at Humières aerodrome near St Pol, May 1918. These young volunteers had come from America, Canada, New Zealand, England and South Africa. Lt C Hooper of the USAS is on the right *(Bruce Robertson)*

Air fighting developed from the need to foil the enemy's aerial attempts to spy on army positions and movements. Here, observer Lt John H Snyder in a Salmson 2A 2 two-seater of the 91st Aero (US) Squadron hands over vital photographic intelligence. In its five months existence (June to November 1918) the 91st Aero lost 13 fliers, but successfully downed 21 enemy aircraft. The 91st's sole ace was observer/gunner W T Badham, who was credited with five victories in company with his pilots (see Chapter 7) (US National Archives)

TACTICS

The Great War was fought in many parts of the world, including northern Italy, Gallipoli (Turkey), Greece, Macedonia, Palestine, Russia, and Bulgaria; but mostly it was fought in France – the Western Front. By and large the Western Front was divided into two main parts. From the Belgium coast south to roughly the city of Amiens, the British and Belgian armies held the line, while the region from Amiens to the Vosges mountains was the responsibility of the French. Each army had its air brigades, wings and squadrons, and men from all Allied nationalities joined the various air forces to fight in the third dimension.

Following the opening battles of 1914, the stalemate began that winter, with the Germans, British and French digging in, creating a line of trench systems which ran from the North Sea coast to Switzerland. The aeroplane was a new innovation in 20th century warfare, but it suddenly became important once the trenches made it impossible for cavalry to make reconnaissance patrols to see what the opposition was up to. It was the airman in his flying machine, soon to be armed with a camera, who alone could bring back this intelligence for the generals.

It was just such airborne reconnaissance that warned the Allies of the inward shift of the Germans' extreme right-flank army so that it would pass to the east of Paris rather than the west as ordained in the Schlieffen Plan. The Allies rearranged their forces accordingly and checked the Germans in the 1st Battle of the Marne, the first German reverse of the war. Closely allied to reconnaissance was artillery observation. The orbiting aircraft spotted the fall of their guns' fire and sent back corrections: initially this was done by dropping messages, but later radio was used.

Air fighting therefore developed from the need to stop each side flying over the trenches in order to 'spy', and the fighter was born. Initially pilots took up service weapons such as rifles and pistols, or even sporting guns, to pot at the enemy before machine guns gradually arrived. Aircraft also began to be used to bomb hostile gun batteries and other targets. So the fighting pilots made a niche for themselves in popular folklore. These new 'knights of the air', a phrase coined by the press, had a certain mystique, a certain aura about them. They became a more deadly type of pop-idol.

THE RACE FOR AIR SUPERIORITY

Americans fighting with the French and British flew a variety of aircraft supplied from both the French Air Service and the RFC. Even after the USA entered the war, fighter units arriving in France brought no aeroplanes with them and had to rely on European-built machines. Thus two US units (17th and 148th Aero Squadrons) attached to the British flew the Sopwith Camel, whilst the rest, operating with the French, were given the Nieuport 28.

Recognising its forces' lack of preparation for war in the air, the US government took the only practical option in the face of its immediate military and naval aviation requirements and decided to order some 5,875 aircraft plus 8,500 aero-engines from the French. (Only a quarter had been delivered by war's end, and the rest were then cancelled). To save precious time, the US also decided to purchase existing French, British and Italian designs rather than give the task to its infant and inexperienced aircraft industry. It did, however, develop the Liberty aero-engine, designed as a type that could be produced in a number of forms, most notably 8- and 12-cylinder Vee units. From early 1918 the flow of American-built Liberty aero-engines to the Allies greatly helped to redress the inbalance between readily available airframes and a serious lack of engines.

The speed with which aircraft were designed and produced in World War 1 was not just impressive, it was near miraculous. In 1914 most

US Army Signal Corps mechanics reassembling Nieuport 17s at Issoudon, France, in May 1917. Issoudon soon became the biggest US flying training school in France. By the time of the Armistice, 16 American flying schools in France were training or retraining some 2,000 pilots every month (US National Archive)

military men considered the aeroplane little more than a curiosity of only marginal practical value. By 1918 it had been developed into a thoroughly practical machine in its many forms. Four years of war had increased technological development to an unprecedented rate.

DELAGE AND THE NIEUPORTS

The Nieuport 11 'Bébé' was designed by Gustave Delage for the Gorden Bennett Trophy air race in August 1914. The race was cancelled because of the outbreak of war, but when the Allies realised that they urgently needed a true fighter to combat the Fokker E.1 monoplane, the 11 seemed an ideal solution. Based on a wooden structure covered largely with fabric, it was a small biplane with a fixed tailskid landing gear and a sesquiplane wing cellule incorporating a single Vee interplane strut on each side. The front-mounted 59.6 kW (80 hp) Le Rhône 9C rotary engine drove a two-blade wooden tractor propeller. The Allies lacked any type of effective gun synchronisation system that would have permitted the installation of a machine gun on the upper part of the forward fuselage to fire through the disc swept by the propeller, and were therefore forced to site a Lewis gun above the upper wing where it could fire right over the propeller, even though this meant that the pilot had to stand up in his cockpit to replace a spent ammunition drum with a fresh unit. The Nieuport 11 initially entered service with the French army air service in the summer of 1916 as the 11C.1 single-seat fighter, and was the type flown by Raoul Lufbery, leading ace of the *Lafayette Escadrille*.

The most successful of the Nieuport single-seat fighters to see service in World War 1, the 17, was a progressive development of 11. It had a more refined airframe, a lengthened sesquiplane wing cellule and a strengthened lower wing in an attempt to defeat the flutter that had troubled earlier Nieuport fighters. As soon as effective gun synchronisation equipment was available, the old, unsatisfactory machine gun installation gave way to a more practical system based on a belt-fed Vickers machine gun on the

This Nieuport 16 had fittings on the outer sides of the two V-type interplane struts for a total of eight Le Prier rockets for use in the 'balloon-busting' role. N959 from *Escadrille* N65 was captured intact by the Germans on 22 May 1916, its French pilot, Adj. Henri Réservat, becoming a PoW

upper part of the forward fuselage immediately ahead of the cockpit. Such was the success of the 17C.1 that the Germans seemed to panic in ordering their aircraft manufacturers to copy the type. It was only with the advent of the Albatros D.I in September 1916 that the Germans finally acquired a generally effective counter to this extremely nimble Nieuport.

The last sesquiplane from Nieuport was the Type 24. Although it did not offer much improvement over the current 17, it was ordered into production for service from June 1917 with the French. The 14bis version, with rectangular wing tips and the more angular tail unit of the 17, was flown by the Americans and the British.

By 1917 most aircraft designers on each side had decided that the air-cooled rotary engine was ready to give way to a water-cooled inline or Vee engine which offered more power. Gustave Delage disagreed. He favoured the lighter and more agile rotary-engined type for the dogfighting role, leaving heavier fighters with water-cooled engines for the dive-and-zoom attack. The Nieuport 28 summarised his whole experience with rotary engined fighters, and provided a useful if not excellent blend of agility and moderately good performance. It was ordered into production for service with the French army air service as the 28C.1, but the French preferred the new SPAD S.XIII.

The 28 was saved from obscurity by the American Expeditionary Force, who were desperate for modern fighters and were grateful to receive 297 aircraft of this type from late February 1918 to equip the 27th, 94th, 95th and 147th Aero Squadrons.

The start of combat operations was postponed into the early part of April by delays in the delivery of guns, which arrived separately from the aircraft, and then by the revelation that the American pilots had received no instruction in air-to-air gunnery. Because of the weapon delays, a

Left to right: Eddie Rickenbacker, the American ace of aces with 26 victories, Doug Campbell (the first US trained pilot to become an ace) and Ken Marr (CO of the 94th Aero) pose in front of a Nieuport 28 (Franks Collection)

Rickenbacker's 'White 12' (N6159). A 'Third Liberty Loan' poster has been pasted to the top starboard wing *(Phil Jarrett)*

number of the aircraft were fitted with American weapons in the form of two 0.3 in (7.62 mm) Marlin guns, while aircraft intended for the 'balloon busting' role were generally fitted with just one 0.433 in (11 mm) Vickers machine gun in the port-side position and firing incendiary ammunition.

American pilots liked the 28C.1's great agility and good climb rate, but became less favourably disposed to the fighter when operations revealed the unreliability of the Gnôme engine and the tendency of the upper wing to shed its fabric covering in tight manoeuvres and/or prolonged dives. Even so, the first victories gained by the air component of the American Expeditionary Force were gained by pilots of the 28C.1 on 14 April, Lieutenants Alan Winslow and Douglas Campbell intercepting a pair of German fighters: Winslow shot down a Pfalz D.III and Campbell forced an Albatros D.Va to crash land.

SPAD: THE FIGHTING STAR

The manufacturer SPAD (the Société Pour l'Aviation et ses Dérivés) introduced its S.VII (or S.7) in mid-1916 as what was for the time a revolutionary fighter. The S.VIIC.1 fighter featured a thin aerofoil section and, unlike earlier French fighters which had used the air-cooled rotary type of engine, boasted a stationary water-cooled Vee engine, the eight-cylinder Hispano-Suiza 8 rated at 150 hp (112 kW).

A SPAD S.VII of French *Escadrille SPA 3* in which Charles Parsons served and in which Frank Baylies served and died *(Bruce Robertson)*

Close-up of the twin Vickers
synchronised machine guns on a
SPAD S.XIII purchased from the
French for the US Air Service
(*Bruce Robertson*)

THE RACE FOR AIR SUPERIORITY

The evolution of the SPAD fighters moved on apace with the introduction of the S.XII (or S.12), which had an even more powerful engine and a 37 mm cannon in addition to the S.VII's single 0.303 in (7.7 mm) machine gun.

The S.XIII (or S.13) was first flown in April 1917. With the future of France then at stake there was no time to spare and it was put into service the following month. Compared with the S.XII, the S.XIII had a wing cellule of slighter greater span, improved ailerons and other streamlining design refinements, plus the synchronised armament of two machine guns.

The S.XIIIC.1 immediately proved to be a superb fighter, and was flown by many leading aces including the American 'ace of aces' Eddie Rickenbacker. The S.XIII was one of the European designs selected by the Americans for mass production in the USA, but in the event all the 893 aircraft of this type delivered to the American Expeditionary Force were purchased directly from the French.

ROYAL AIRCRAFT FACTORY:
S.E.5/S.E.5A

Taking into account the minimum flying training given to novice pilots in the heat of World War 1, it was crucial that any new fighter should be easy to fly. It also needed to be easy to manufacture. The S.E.5, a single-seat biplane, first flew in November 1916 and had entered service by April 1917. Although not as manoeuvrable as its famous contemporary, the Sopwith Camel, it proved to be fast, sturdy and viceless in its handling. Its two machine guns were located in a somewhat odd arrangement as one Vickers weapon in the upper part of the fuselage and one Lewis gun over the upper-wing's centre section.

Many S.E.5a's were supplied for the US Air Service who adapted the roundel form for national identity with a white centre, blue inner and red outer. Numbers were shipped to the USA post-war *(Bruce Robertson)*

A key feature in the Camel's agility was the location of all the major masses in the short forward fuselage around the centre of gravity. It also made it difficult to handle, as many inexperienced pilots found to their cost *(MARS)*

The S.E.5 was powered by a new 150 hp (112 kW) Hispano-Suiza 8 engine. The change to an inadequately developed 200 hp (149 kW) geared version of the same engine for the S.E.5a resulted in problems as the engine was unreliable. Nevertheless, the S.E.5a matured into one of the finest British fighters of the war after it had been fitted with the Wolseley Viper, which was a high-compression development of the original French engine. The S.E.5a proved more than a match for the Fokker D.VII and Pfalz D.XII fighters it encountered in 1918 (see Chapter 4 for details of American S.E.5 aces flying with the RFC and RAF).

SOPWITHS

Small but extremely fast and powerful and with a phenomenal rate of climb, the single-seater Sopwith Triplane fighter impressed from the start. In summer 1916 it was put into large-scale production for the RNAS and RFC but political prevarication held production back. In the end less than 150 were built and flown, exclusively by the RNAS. The first triplane to be used on the Western Front, it dominated the skies and struck terror into its adversaries for a brief seven months before being superseded by the Sopwith Camel. O C 'Boots' Le Boutillier from New Jersey flying with the 9 Naval Squadron downed four enemy aircraft with the Triplane in the summer of 1917.

The Sopwith Camel first flew in March 1917 and entered service in May with RFC and RNAS squadrons. By early 1918 there were enough American pilots in service with the RAF to form two all-American fighter squadrons flying the Camel: the 17th and the 148th Aero (see Chapter 5).

Like its predecessor, the Pup, the Camel soon gained a nickname which has long survived the official Sopwith Biplane F.1 designation of the initial production version. The Camel is rightly regarded as the finest British fighter of World War 1, and was without doubt the most successful air combat aeroplane in terms of the numbers of aircraft it shot down. Somewhat heavier than the Sopwith Pup, the Camel was powered by

The Camel was the most successful British fighter of World War 1. It is seen here in the form of an F.1 fighter, the initial production version, which was fitted with a 110 hp (82 kW) Clerget rotary engine (MARS)

Lt Laurence T Wyly in a Sopwith F.I Camel of the 148th Aero. Wyly was wounded on 15 August 1918, and had his Camel shot-up on 29 October *(Phil Jarrett)*

engines of 100 to 150 hp (75 to 112 kW) by Bentley, Clerget, Gnôme and Le Rhône, and had all its major masses (armament, fuel, pilot and engine) concentrated within the forward 7 ft (1.13 m) of the fuselage, a concentration of major masses on and around the centre of gravity that resulted in outstanding manoeuvrability. This was enhanced by the torque of the large engine and propeller, making possible snap turns to starboard which were so fast that some pilots would make a three-quarter starboard instead of a one-quarter port turn. Not only did they believe this to be faster in combat, but it was tactically confusing to an enemy pilot. On the other hand, it should be noted, this tendency also made the Camel very tricky to land, and accidents were all too frequent.

A Sopwith 5F.1 Dolphin showing the two upward-firing Lewis guns attached to a crossbar mounting over the cockpit. The American Expeditionary Force acquired five examples of the type *(Hawker)*

The Sopwith 5F Dolphin first flew in May 1917, and by the end of the year 121 aircraft had been delivered to the RFC. Having been developed as a high-altitude single-seat fighter, in the event it became a close air support machine, with trench and ground strafing as its primary role. The 200 hp geared Hispano-Suiza engine was troublesome, as was the revolutionary crossbar mounting of two upward-firing Lewis guns, which had an urge to swing round and strike the pilot in the face. Since the Dolphin also possessed twin, synchronised Vickers guns, the crossbar guns were mostly done away with.

Bristol F2.Bs of 22 Squadron RFC at Vert Galand, 1 April 1918. In the foreground is C4810. These aircraft were built by the British & Colonial Aircraft Co *(Bruce Robertson)*

'BRISFIT'

The prototype of the two-seater Bristol Fighter, affectionately known as the 'Brisfit', first flew in September 1916 and delivery of the first 50 F.2As had already started by the end of December. Powered by a Rolls-Royce Falcon engine, its armament consisted of a Lewis gun mounted in the rear cockpit and a 0.303 in (7.7 mm) Vickers machine gun mounted on the centreline beneath the engine cowling, which meant that a tunnel had to be designed through the upper-fuselage fuel tank.

No. 48 Squadron, the first RFC Squadron to re-equip with the F.2A, received its first aircraft in February 1917 and flew them to France on 8 March. Meanwhile, a further 200 of the new, improved F.2B version had been ordered with modifications which included an improved pilot's view, an enlarged fuel tank, a bigger ammunition box for the Vickers gun and a possible bomb load of up to 240 lb. Later F.2Bs were given the 275 hp Falcon III engine, giving them a speed of 125 mph at sea level and a ceiling of 20,000 ft. Over 3,000 F.2Bs had been built by the end of 1918.

Initially, Bristol Fighters were used as gun platforms for their observers with disastrous results. Very quickly pilots realised that the aircraft should be used as a single seater, with the forward-firing Vickers gun used as the main armament. From that moment the 'Brisfit' became one of the most effective – and indeed legendary – fighters of its day. A number of Americans flew 'Brisfits' both solo and with an observer, notably Wilfred Beaver, E S Coler, the Iaccaci brothers August and Paul, and Walter K Simon.

AMERICANS FLYING WITH THE FRENCH

By 1915 there were a number of American men serving France in various capacities and some had become interested in aviation. During the first couple of years of the war, the aeroplane had caught the imagination of many young men, especially those who saw little future in the mud and brutal death of the trenches that carved their hideous scars across the French landscape from the North Sea coast to Switzerland.

Once it began to be mooted that perhaps it was possible to group together those Americans interested in fighting France's enemies in the air, the question of neutrality was naturally raised. The only way American nationals could fight for France was to enlist through the French Foreign Legion, from where those who wanted to fly, and not to fight in the trenches, were guided into the French flight training system.

It is interesting, but not particularly helpful, to note that the French squadron (*escadrille*) designations 'N' and 'SPA' although referring to Nieuport and SPAD did not necessarily mean that the *escadrille* only flew one type. *Escadrilles* often operated both; it also took a while for headquarters to change the designation from N to SPA when an *escadrille* re-equipped.

THE *LAFAYETTE ESCADRILLE*

The story of the Lafayette Squadron, officially *Escadrille* N 124, has gone into legend. There were enough American airmen wanting to fight with

A two-seater Voisin bomber of the pusher type that Raoul Lufbery flew with *Escadrille* VB106 for six months before his transfer to fighters. Vulnerable in daylight, they were mostly used for night bombing. In those early days, light bombs or darts *(flèchettes)* were carried in the cockpit and thrown over the side *(Bruce Robertson)*

V. 1817

Nieuport 17s of the *Lafayette Escadrille*. Note the squadron's 'Seminole' Indian head emblem on the fuselage. The squadron's founder, Norman Prince, and other *Lafayette* members, including Raoul Lufbery, James McConnell and Kiffen Rockwell, were all to die in combat *(US National Archives)*

Top ace of the *Lafayette Escadrille* (N 124) was Gervais Raoul Lufbery, with 17 victories. He scored his first victory on 30 July 1916 and became the first American *Lafayette* ace on 12 October by shooting down a Roland two-seater *(Bruce Robertson)*

the French to form a complete squadron so, led by the squadron's creator, lawyer Norman Prince, they were grouped together and on 16 April 1916 formed the *Escadrille Americaine*. The name caused a stir in German diplomatic circles and it was soon changed to the *Lafayette Escadrille* (a salute to the inspirational French general who offered his services to the American Revolutionaries in their War of Independence). Led by a French CO and French flight commanders, the squadron went to the front in April 1915 where it remained on active duty until it was disbanded in February 1918 to become the American 103rd Aero Squadron. Its French and American pilots saw much combat during 1916–17, claiming over 40 victories. Many of its American pilots made names for themselves, names that went into history and folklore. However, it only produced one air ace, Gervais Raoul Lufbery.

Although Raoul Lufbery's father was an American, Lufbery was born in France of a French mother on 14 March 1885, so was older than many of his contemporaries in N 124. By 1916 he already had a lifetime of adventure behind him, having run away from home at 17, travelling to Algeria, Tunisia, Egypt, Turkey and the Balkans. In 1906 he finally saw America, joined the army and saw active duty in the Philippines. Later he travelled to China, Japan and India, seeing his first aeroplane in Cochin, China, in 1910. He made the acquaintance of a French pilot in Calcutta in 1912 and became his mechanic. In August 1914, the pilot volunteered his aeroplane and himself to the service of France and Lufbery went too – via the Foreign Legion.

His pilot did not survive long, and upon his death Lufbery joined the Air Service himself and became a pilot, flying two-seater bombers. But once N 124 was formed, he was transferred to it to join his American half-brothers flying the Nieuport 11. From mid-1916 until the end of 1917 he became a formidable air fighter, being credited with 16 official victories plus a further 13 probables, rising from Sergent to Sous-lieutenant, and winning the Médaille Militaire, the Légion d'Honneur and the Croix de Guerre with ten palms, while the British awarded him their Military Medal.

Like many of France's top air aces, he was fêted the hero, and then in late 1917, with the arrival of the American Air Service in France, he was commissioned into the USAS and given command of the 94th Pursuit

Bill Thaw gained his first victory with the *Lafayette Escadrille,* a Fokker Eindecker on 24 May 1916, and made ace once the *Escadrille* became the 103rd Squadron USAS in 1918, which he also commanded *(Bruce Robertson)*

Ed Parsons in the uniform of SPA 3 in the *Cigognes* Group. Parsons also flew with the *Lafayette Escadrille* achieving one victory before moving to the elite SPA 3 where he stayed for the duration of the war. He had eight official victories confirmed *(E F Cheesman)*

David Peterson claimed one victory with the *Lafayette,* three with the 94th and two with the 95th Pursuit Squadrons to make ace, commanding the latter unit in 1918. He is pictured here standing by a Nieuport 28 of the 94th *(Bruce Robertson)*

Squadron. As this unit was working up for combat, Major Lufbery had several encounters with enemy aircraft but did not add to his score. Attacking a German two-seater on 19 May 1918, his Nieuport 28 was set on fire by a burst from the German observer. Like so many other World War 1 aviators faced with a fiery death, he chose to jump from the flames, and fell to his death. He was 33.

While Lufbery was the only *Lafayette* ace, other pilots from the squadron did become aces later on, one being William Thaw. Born 12 August 1893, he came from Pittsburg, and had actually flown pre-war, while still at Yale University. When war came he joined the Foreign Legion and saw active duty with the infantry before volunteering as an air gunner on French two-seater aircraft. From here he progressed to pilot, and his courage brought him a field commission. His CO, Georges Thenault, when given command of the new N 124, obviously had the American assigned.

With N 124 Thaw gained two official victories and at least two probables. He too won the Légion d'Honneur and the Croix de Guerre, and was wounded once. Thaw also transferred to the USAS and took command of the squadron as it became the 103rd Aero. Leading them he gained three further victories, adding the DSC and Oak Leaf Cluster to his chest of medals. After the war he went into the aviation industry in Pittsburg but died of pneumonia on 22 April 1934.

Two other aces, Edwin C Parsons and David Peterson, opened their scoring with the *Lafayette.* Both claimed one official victory, and ended the war with eight and six respectively. Parsons, born on 24 September 1892, came from Holyoke, Massachusetts, and was almost 22 as the war began. Between 1913 and 1915 he had seen active duty with the Mexican Army Aviation Corps, having learnt to fly in Los Angeles. He went to France with the Ambulance Service, then volunteered for aviation, ending up with the *Lafayette Escadrille.* Although he flew with it for many months his only victory came in September 1917. Home leave was granted over the winter of 1917–18, and in the new year he transferred to the elite SPA 3 of the French Air Service. Over the summer of 1918

he brought his score to eight, while his decorations included the Médaille Militaire, Croix de Guerre with 8 palms, Belgium War Cross, and the Belgian Order of Léopold, he also received the Medal of the Aero Club of America. After the war he became an FBI agent, went to Hollywood to advise on several aviation films, and finally in 1940 became a Lieutenant-Commander in the US Navy. He saw active service in the Solomons in World War 2 ending up as a Rear-Admiral. He died on 2 May 1968 in Florida, having received the French Légion d'Honneur seven years earlier.

Born 2 July 1895, David McKelvey Peterson came from Pennsylvania, and joined the French Air Service in October 1916. He flew with N 124 the following summer. After gaining his first victory he transferred to the USAS and, as a Captain, served with the 94th Aero, scoring three further victories before being given command of the 95th, where he brought his

Ed Parsons' *Lafayette* Nieuport 17 after Kenneth Marr (who never made ace but later became CO of the 94th) overshot on landing and came to an undignified halt on a railway embankment
(Franks Collection)

Lafayette pilot Robert Soubiran by his Indian-Head marked SPAD
(Phil Jarrett)

score to six. He won the DSC and Oak Leaf Cluster and returned to the US as the war ended. He was killed in a flying accident at Daytona, Florida, on 16 March 1919.

THE LAFAYETTE FLYING CORPS

As the war progressed, more American volunteers arrived to swell the ranks of N 124 but an *escadrille* can only have so many pilots, so in order to accommodate the extra flyers, these pilots were sent to other French units. However, to embrace all American volunteers with the French, they were collectively known as members of the Lafayette Flying Corps. Many of these men, following experience with various French *escadrilles,* transferred to the USAS in 1918, but quite a number, just like Ed Parsons, elected to remain with the French. One of these was David Endicott Putnam.

From Jamaica Plains, Massachusetts, David Putnam, born 10 December 1898, was a descendant of General Isaac Putnam of Revolutionary fame. He volunteered for aviation while still under age, so he sailed to France and joined the French Air Service while still only 18. His first unit was SPA 94 in December 1917, the month he was 19. Putnam gained his first victory on 19 January 1918 shortly after going to *Escadrille* MS 156. He was always to be found in the thick of the fighting, and by the beginning of June, while he had four official victories, the young daredevil had at least another eight which had not

A SPAD S.VII of SPA 3. All four *Escadrilles* of *Groupe de Combat 12* carried a different *cigogne* (stork) emblem on their aircraft, of which SPA 3's emblem was the most famous. The *Cigognes* considered themselves the élite of French fighter groups *(Bruce Robertson)*

David Putnam was one of the American volunteers sent to other French units when the all-American *Lafayette Escadrille* could take no more pilots. He flew with French Squadrons in 1917–18 scoring nine official victories to which he added a further four whilst serving with the 139th Aero. A fearless fighter, at least eight more victories could not be confirmed because he had been so far over the enemy lines. His luck ran out on 12 September 1918, when he was shot down and killed by the German ace, Georg von Hantelmann *(Bruce Robertson)*

been confirmed because he had been so far over the other side of the German lines.

Putnam then went to SPA 38 where his aggressive mode of fighting continued. On 5 June he claimed five victories but only one was confirmed, and on the 14th he and another pilot claimed three more but two of these were unconfirmed. (There had to be at least two other pilots to confirm a kill in the French system of confirmations.) Towards the end of June 1918 Putnam transferred into the USAS and, as acting CO of the 139th Pursuit, brought his score to 13 confirmed, plus many unconfirmed. Some say his score was as high as 34, had he been able to confirm kills, which would have made him the American top ace, but he appears to have been more concerned with downing his opponents than having his score approved.

Frank Baylies was another American to do well with the elite SPA 3, gaining 12 victories in 1918 before his own death in combat against Fokker Triplanes of *Jasta 19* on 17 June *(E F Cheesman)*

The French had given him the Médaille Militaire and the Croix de Guerre, and after his death in combat, the Légion d'Honneur. He was killed in action on 12 September 1918, shot down by the German ace Georg von Hantelmann, the German's 8th victory of an eventual 25. He was recommended for the Medal of Honour, but only received the DSC, in April 1919, five months after the war had ended, and seven months after his death. In a letter to his mother, Putnam wrote:

'Mother, there is no question about the hereafter of men who give themselves in such a cause. If I am called to make it, I shall go with a grin of satisfaction and a smile.'

Another Lafayette Flying Corps ace was Frank L Baylies, also from Massachusetts – New Bedford – born 23 September 1895. He became a natural and gifted fighter pilot, getting into the Flying Corps via the Ambulance Service, with which he saw active duty in France and Salonika. He won the Croix de Guerre for evacuating wounded under fire in March 1917. A French airman took him up for a flight and soon afterwards he volunteered for aviation, and became a pilot. Like Parsons, he was sent to the prestigious SPA 3 in the Storks Group and began scoring in February 1918. In all he shot down 12 German aircraft, and although he initially refused a commission with the USAS, he eventually took one, but remained with the French *escadrille*. He was killed in action with Fokker Triplanes of *Jasta 19* on 17 June, having received the Médaille Militaire and six palms and one star to his Croix de Guerre.

Charles J Biddle was another American to fly with the French, and another son of Pennsylvania, being born in Andalusia on 13 May 1890, later living in Philadelphia. A graduate of Princeton in 1911 at 21, and Harvard three years later, he was admitted to the Pennsylvania Bar. However, war interrupted his legal career, so he joined the French Air Service and flew with SPA 73 in the famous Storks Group in late 1917 (one victory). He remained with the French despite a

Charles Biddle, a seven-victory ace, first flew with the French, then the *Lafayette Escadrille,* and finally as CO of the 13th Aero. *(Bruce Robertson)*

Nieuport 17 (s/n N1803). Note that because of the small lower wing area, many Nieuports had roundels marked on the top wing undersurfaces (*Bruce Robertson*)

commission into the USAS, but in 1918 finally moved to the 103rd Aero, serving until wounded in May, but having brought his score to three. He returned to the front a month later as commander of the 13th Aero, and with this unit brought his score to seven by the war's end, by which time he had just taken command of the American 4th Pursuit Group. He won the DSC, Purple Heart, French Légion d'Honneur and Croix de Guerre with three palms, plus the Belgian Order of Léopold. After a life in law, he died in Bucks County, PA, on 22 March 1972.

Thomas G Cassady came from Indiana, although born in Iowa on 5 January 1896. Graduating from Chicago University he went to France with the Ambulance Service, then the Foreign Legion in order to transfer into aviation, in July 1917. Assigned to the 103rd Aero, then SPA 163, he gained five official victories and several unconfirmed by August, and was then transferred to the 28th Aero as a flight commander. By the end of the war he had nine victories, the DSC and Oak Leaf Cluster, Légion d'Honneur and the Croix de Guerre with three palms and one star. After

the war he went into the investment business in Chicago. During World War 2 he was with OSS, operating under cover in Vichy France, making four spying trips into France. Later captured as Vichy was occupied by the Germans in 1942, he eventually secured his freedom, only to work for OSS in Algiers to help with the invasion of Southern France. Once Paris was liberated he was put in charge of all intelligence personnel there. He lived till 9 July 1972, dying of cancer, aged 76.

Tom Cassady became an ace flying with the French, adding four more to make nine in all with the 28th Pursuit. In addition to his French decorations, he wears the DSC with Oak Leaf Cluster (*Bruce Robertson*)

Another American who hailed from Philadelphia was James Alexander Connelly Jr, born in

While Gorman deFreest Larner was flying with the French *Escadrille* SPA 86, a fellow pilot plunged to his death in this SPAD S.VII, No 13, accidentaly shot down by friendly fire *(Bruce Robertson)*

Gorman deFreest Larner enlisted into the Lafayette Flying Corps in July 1917 and had gained his wings by September. He was assigned to SPA 86 and scored two kills with the French, adding five more after transferring to the US 103rd Squadron. The first two ribbons on his chest are the DSC with Oak Leaf Cluster, and the Croix de Guerre with two palms *(US National Archives via Bruce Robertson)*

1895. He too went into French aviation via the Foreign Legion, and became a pilot in late 1917. His first assignment was to SPA 157 where he downed an aircraft and a balloon, but then in June moved to SPA 163. By the war's finalé, he had brought his score to seven, plus at least two unconfirmed – all with the French – and received the Médaille Militaire and the Croix de Guerre, as well as the DSC from his own country. He died in New York on 2 February 1944.

James D Beane came from New York City, born 20 January 1896. He went to Concord High School and then worked in Boston before joining the US Ambulance Service. Once in France he saw duty on the French Verdun front from July 1916 to July 1917. He volunteered for duty with French aviation, trained with the *Lafayette Escadrille,* and was then sent to SPA 69 till February 1918, was commissioned into the USAS, but continued with SPA 69. Wounded in June, he lost two fingers and received the Croix de Guerre. Beane then moved to US 22nd Aero and flying SPADs, and shot down six German aircraft before his death in combat on 30 October. He received a posthumous DSC.

Charles Gossage Grey, from Chicago, was born on 20 June 1894. He joined the Lafayette Flying Corps in July 1917 and went to SPA 93 in November, serving with this unit until March the following year. Commissioned into the USAS he was assigned to the 203rd Pursuit Squadron on

William T Ponder, standing in front of a SPAD. Three victories with the French and three more with the 103rd Pursuit brought him acedom in 1918 *(E F Cheesman)*

1 August as a flight commander. He achieved five victories and won the DSC. He was killed in 1984, the result of a hit-and-run auto-accident, in Palm Beach, California.

Gorman deFreest Larner, from New York, was born in Washington DC on 5 July 1897. Trying to join the Air Service he was deemed too young so he travelled to France and was accepted into the French Air Service in July 1917. In December he was assigned to SPA 86 claiming two victories in March 1918. Commissioned into the USAS in April he remained with the French until June, at which time he was sent to the 103rd Aero as a flight commander. By the end of the war he had brought his victory score to seven, and had won the DSC with Oak Leaf Cluster and the French Croix de Guerre with two Palms. Made captain on 8 November Larner served on the American staff during the Paris Peace Conference before returning home in September 1919.

After completing his education at Columbia University he went into banking, but in World War 2 he became a colonel in the USAAC Reserve. After that conflict he became General Manager of the National Aeronautical Association and Chairman of Robinson Aviation Inc., in Teterboro, New Jersey. He retired in 1964 and died in Easton, Connecticut on, 20 May 1984.

William T Ponder came from Mangum, Oklahoma, and joined the French Air Service in the autumn of 1917. His first French *escadrille* was SPA 67, then SPA 163 in May 1918. With this unit he claimed three victories, but then received a commission into the USAS and moved to the 103rd Aero in September. Ponder added another three kills to his total, bringing his score to six, and with this came the DSC. He died of a heart ailment at Amarillo, Texas, on 27 February 1947.

Yet another ace from New York was Remington deB Vernam, born 24 March 1896. With the French he flew with SPA 96, gaining one official victory – a balloon – on 12 August 1918. Commissioned into the USAS he joined the 22nd Aero, added five more to his tally and won the DSC. On 30 October he was shot down in combat into the German lines. Badly wounded, he was abandoned by the retreating Germans and when found by units of the Red Cross he was very ill and died of his injuries on 1 December.

AMERICANS FLYING WITH THE BRITISH

American fighter pilots who fought with the British fell into two categories. Firstly, those who decided to fight for France and Britain in the air, before America came into the war on 6 April 1917, and those who, having joined the American Air Service after that date, trained either in America or with the British in Canada or England, and were sent to British squadrons to gain experience. Once they had gained this experience of actual combat, the plan was to send them to American squadrons as they began to arrive in France during 1918.

It has to be said that at the time America came into the war 'Uncle Sam' had no combat aircraft of his own, and almost none of the commanders of the embryo service had any combat experience, and no doubt its training programme reflected this too. Thus many young men who felt they should join the colours, having chosen flight as their way of fighting, quickly realised that it would be far better to train under experienced instructors and be guaranteed at least an aircraft that gave a chance of survival against an equally experienced German air force. These men made straight for Canada, or even Britain, to join the RFC and RNAS.

Britain certainly welcomed the additional surge of recruits into its flying services, but even before this influx, there had been men who had been with the British prior to April 1917. One of the most notable, not only for his combat record, but also because he was among the first Americans to fight with the RFC, was Frederick Libby from Sterling, Colorado, born 15 July 1891. This western cowboy was 23 years of age in August 1914, and almost straight away journeyed to Canada and joined the army, arriving in France in 1915. After some months in the hell of the trenches, he volunteered for the RFC following a call for men to act as air gunners. These air gunners were actually known as observers, due to the fact that only part of their job was to man a machine gun in order to defend their aircraft from air attack. The other job often involved 'observing' movement of troops, trains, cavalry on the ground, or to spot German artillery and machine gun positions.

Fred Libby was assigned to No 23 Squadron RFC, flying an FE 2b 'pusher' type aircraft. That is, the engine was 'in-back', pushing the craft, rather than in front like the 'tractor' type, whose engine and propeller pulled the machine through the air. Libby was therefore stuck out in the front cockpit of the gondola, where the observer had a wide field of fire with his Lewis machine gun, and a rather precarious position if he had to stand up and fire a second gun fixed to a pole, and set to fire back over the top wing. Nevertheless, he survived combats in the summer of 1916, and even managed to shoot down and destroy a German two-seater on 15 July for his first kill. Libby then moved to No 11 Squadron, another unit flying the big FE 2 aeroplanes, and for the rest of that summer and into the

Like many observers, Fred Libby was not trained to be a pilot. In 1917 he rectified the situation and saw a wealth of action with four RFC squadrons both as an observer and a pilot. He flew the somewhat primitive but effective FE 2b as an observer, and graduated to the Sopwith 11/2 Strutter before moving on to No 25 Squadron. flying the Airco D.H.4 bomber and ending the war with a grand total of 14 victories *(E F Cheesman)*

27

autumn, he and his pilots accounted for a further nine German aircraft, all claimed as 'out of control'.

Perhaps here we should mention the way victories were assessed during World War 1. If an opposing aeroplane was seen to fall in flames, or in pieces, or crash, or perhaps the pilot was seen to fall or jump out, then that counted as a *destroyed*. If an aeroplane, once attacked, appeared to fall from the sky, usually in a spin, but not actually be seen to hit the ground or fall apart, this was noted as an *out of control victory* (in World War 2 it would have been classed as a *probable*). Obviously there was no certain way of knowing if, once low down or perhaps having spun out of sight through cloud, the enemy pilot righted his machine and flew home, as many would have done. So it could only be assumed to have crashed. Confirmation from other pilots or even ground observers would have to be fairly certain that, to all intents and purposes, the falling machine appeared to have crashed for the attacking pilot to have this 'victory' acknowledged.

By the very nature of the First World War, where the British almost always were fighting over the German side of the front lines, confirmation of crashes was not always easy, and not every aircraft attacked would go down in flames or begin to disintegrate. So in order to assess the successful result of a combat, the *out of control* victory was allowed. Therefore, a pilot or an observer's tally of victories might include a number of destroyed AND 'out of control' claims. The French, and then the Americans, only acknowledged aircraft actually seen to be destroyed in a pilot's score, citations noting these, and only mentioning 'probables' in passing. Sometimes, however, these probables had been destroyed, but without any witnesses from air or ground, a destroyed/confirmed victory would not be allowed. Many French pilots flying 'lone wolf' patrols often had a string of probables, as they fought alone and therefore had nobody to corroborate their claims. The British got round this by allowing probables – 'out of controls' – to be added to a pilot's score.

So, although Fred Libby, with 11 Squadron, claimed nine victories, all appear to be of the 'out of control' variety, although without doubt, a number would have crashed. This in no way diminishes his or any other airman's claims to victories, it was the system used in World War 1, and everyone understood it. For his work with 11 Squadron, Libby was awarded the Military Cross and, like many other observers, realised that he too could pilot an aeroplane, so requested formal training, although he had already had several unofficial training flights with his various pilots. Sent to England, he successfully completed a flying course, and in March 1917 was back in France as a pilot.

He was posted to No 43 Squadron, which flew the Sopwith 1¹/₂ Strutter (which the French used too and called the Sopwith two-seater). This was a tractor machine, with the observer, more conventionally, in the rear cockpit. This squadron was also a fighting unit, using its ability to stay in combat with German fighters to fight its way to bomb targets, to

The Royal Aircraft Factory FE 2b was designed as a two-seater multi-role fighter, reconnaissance aircraft and night bomber. Up front was the observer/gunner with a Lewis machine gun, behind and above him sat the pilot, and behind the pilot were the engine and propeller 'pushing' the aircraft along. With a top speed of 91.5 mph at sea level, it was not exactly fast but it was certainly effective, particularly as a night bomber, right through to 1918. Fred Libby, one of the first Americans to sign up with the RFC, claimed nine victories flying the FE 2b with No 11 Sqn as an observer/air gunner *(Dowty Boulton Paul)*

Fred Libby completed his victory tally by adding two enemy aircraft to his score in August 1917 flying the D.H.4 bomber with No 25 Squadron. The D.H.4 was generally agreed to be the finest day bomber to see large-scale service during the Great War, and was also the only British aeroplane of its time to be built in large numbers in the USA (fitted with the Liberty Vee engine). In all 1,885 were shipped to France for use by the American Expeditionary Forces, although only about one-third of them were used operationally *(US National Archives)*

Clive Warman arrived at No 23 Sqn in June 1917 to fly SPAD VIIs and notched up his 12 victories in less than two months. On 16 August, his guns jammed while in combat, so he fired off his Very flares at his attackers, and as a last resort hurled his wooden cockpit hammer at them – and lived to tell the tale *(E F Cheesman)*

photograph important areas, or to reconnoitre any given location. Libby added two further victories to his tally, and then went to 25 Squadron, flying D.H.4 bombers. During August 1917 he and his observers downed two more hostile aircraft, bringing Libby's total claims to 14. He was also the first American to become an ace in World War 1.

With the rank of Captain, Libby transferred to the USAS in September 1917, was sent on a fund-raising tour of the States, and was then assigned to the 22nd Pursuit Squadron at Hicks Field. However, he became ill with a circulation and spinal impairment which made him unfit for further flying duties, and in fact remained a partial cripple for the rest of his life. America's first ace died in Los Angeles, on 9 January 1970, having survived to his 78th year.

In 1917, No 23 Squadron, in which Libby had flown FE 2s, had converted to single-seat SPAD VIIs, purchased from the French. In mid-summer, Clive Wilson Warman, from Norfolk, West Virginia, where he had been born on 30 June 1892, arrived to fly SPADs with this unit. Clive Warman had been a civil engineer pre-war, but enlisted into the Princess Patricia's Canadian Light Infantry in Canada, sailing to England in January 1915. Going to France he was wounded in the Second Battle of Ypres that April, and after recovering went to Ireland where he was involved in the Easter Rebellion in Dublin the following year.

That summer, back in England, he transferred into the RFC and was commissioned. On completion of his flight training, he was selected to

29

be an instructor, so it was not until June 1917 that he achieved his aim to join a fighting squadron – going to No 23. His skill as a pilot was equally matched as a marksman and in less than two months he had achieved 12 victories and won not only the Military Cross, but the Distinguished Service Order. Among his victories were two observation balloons, targets that were also added to a pilot's score in World War 1. Of his ten aeroplane victories, eight were noted as confirmed destroyed. In one of his last combats, on 16 August, his guns jammed whilst in a fight with three enemy fighters. Rather than breaking off the fight, he fired off his Very flares at them, then in sheer desperation, hurled the wooden hammer he kept in his cockpit to help with gun jams. Four days later he was wounded in combat and forced down, fortunately inside Allied lines. He was under medical care until mid-1918 and then went to Air Ministry in London, not seeing further action. After the war he became a flight commander with the new No 1 Canadian Squadron, near Edmonton, Alberta, but on 8 May 1919 he was seriously injured in a crash, and died on 12 June.

Another ace who started his fighting career early was Oliver Colin LeBoutillier – known as 'Boots'. 'Boots' came from Montclair, New Jersey, born 24 May 1895. He went north to Canada in August 1916 and joined the RNAS. Following pilot training he went to France to join 9 Naval Squadron, flying the Sopwith Triplane fighter. In the summer of 1917 he downed four enemy aircraft 'out of control'. In the new year, 9 Naval re-equipped with the agile Sopwith Camel, and then on 1 April his outfit became 209 Squadron RAF when the RFC and RNAS amalgamated to form the Royal Air Force.

His next victory, his fifth, and the first with the Camel, was an Albatros two-seater which crashed at Beaucourt, in the opening sequence of events which ended in the death of German's top ace, Baron Manfred von

Oliver 'Boots' LeBoutillier gained his first four victories flying the Sopwith Triplane with No 9 Naval Squadron RNAS in 1917. Re-equipped with Camels he brought his score to ten in 1918, No 9 Naval having become No 209 Squadron RAF *(Franks collection)*

The Sopwith Triplanes of the RNAS played a significant part in the operations known as Third Ypres in the summer of 1917. Their reputation was such that the Germans frantically tried to develop a better triplane (Hawker)

Wilfred Beaver (right) claimed 19 combat victories flying two-seater F.2B Bristol Fighters with No 20 Squadron in 1917–18 (E F Cheesman)

Richthofen, who had been in combat with 209 following the first encounter with the two-seater. The next day he and three other pilots brought down another two-seater, which fell into the British lines. In May he claimed a further four victories, bringing his score to ten, by which time he had become a flight commander. By the end of the war he had over 600 flying hours in his flying log book, yet strangely he was not decorated. Returning to America he became a skywriter and later an official in the Skywriting Corporation of America. He also became a stunt flyer, working for the film studios in Hollywood, and also flew in the National Air Races. When Amelia Earhart, the famous aviatrix, started to learn the art of flight, it was 'Boots' who gave her her first dual instruction on a twin-engined aeroplane. In 1937 he was a member of the Civil Aeronautics Corporation, and during World War 2 was the inspector in charge of aviation of Colorado and Wyoming. By the end of his flying career he had over 19,000 hours to his name. He retired to Las Vegas where he died on 12 May 1983.

ROYAL FLYING CORPS/ROYAL AIR FORCE 1918

By far the most American aces to see action with the British had their combat actions in the final year of the war. They were to fly the whole ambit of British fighter types, not only in France but in Italy too.

Wilfred Beaver, for instance, flew Bristol F.2B two-seat fighters. Born on 10 May 1897, he was living in Montreal, Canada, when war came. Joining the RFC, he found himself posted to 20 Squadron in late 1917. He became a flight commander, won the Military Cross and, with his various observer/gunners, claimed an impressive 19 German aircraft shot down before being rested in June 1918. He died on 19 August 1986 in West Point, Mississippi.

Eugene Seeley Coler came from New Jersey, born on 13 January 1896. He joined the RFC in Canada and found himself with No.11 Squadron in 1918. Before being wounded on 16 September he and his observers had accounted for 16 hostile aeroplanes, and Coler received the DFC. He

31

became a doctor after the war with a practice in New York. In World War 2 he served in the 8th Air Force (Major) with the medical branch, and again in the early 1950s in England as a Colonel, but died while in the UK in August 1953. He also held the Legion of Merit and the Bronze Star.

Two other successful American 'Brisfit' aces were in fact New York brothers, August and Paul Iaccaci. It is somewhat amazing that neither men are terribly well known, although they were unique in both being in the same British squadron – No 20. Both achieved 17 victories (between May and September 1918), and both won the DFC. August was made a flight commander with No 48 Squadron in September 1918, but a slight eye wound ended his career before he was able to add to his score. Paul was the first to score: a Fokker Triplane on 18 May, August gaining his first kill the next day over a Pfalz DIII. Paul lived until August 1965, dying in Darien, Connecticut.

Walter K Simon also flew Bristols, but in Italy, under Major W G Barker's command – 139 Squadron. All his claims fell during July 1918, except his last one which he shot down on 10 August (five of them went down on 30 July), in company with his observer, Lt W W Smith. He received the British DFC and then the American DSC.

S.E.5 ACES

Along with the Sopwith Camel, the S.E.5 single-seater scout were the two main British fighters on the Western Front from mid-1917 till the end of the war. It was often pot-luck which fighter type a pilot was sent to so Americans in the RFC/RAF could go to either a Camel or an S.E.5 outfit following training.

Pilots and observers of No 22 Squadron flying Bristol Fighters hand over the contents of their pockets to the orderly officer before taking off for a patrol over the lines. This was a precautionary measure to prevent information reaching the enemy in the event of a forced landing

Two-seater Bristol Fighters 'Brisfits' played a notable part in the air war, especially when flown as single-seaters. Here 22 Squadron are seen taking off from Serny in June 1918

Louis Bennett Jr had a brief but meteoric month flying S.E.5s with No 40 Squadron. August 1918 saw him burn nine balloons and shoot down three aircraft before he too fell in action on 24 August, dying from his injuries after leaping to the ground from his burning aircraft *(E F Cheesman)*

Dealing with American aces in British service in alphabetical sequence, Hilbert Leigh Bair was born in New York on 15 November 1894 and joined the USAS in July 1917. Attached to the RAF for experience he was sent to 24 Squadron on 5 July 1918 and gained six victories (four shared) between 10 August and 15 September, which brought him the award of the British DFC. In October he transferred to the 25th Pursuit, USAS, and was subsequently awarded the American DSC. During World War 2 he was a lieutenant-colonel in the USAAC. He died in White Plains, New York, 24 November 1985.

Louis Bennett Jr, from West Virginia, had a brief but amazing career over the Western Front. Born on 22 September 1894 in the town of Weston, he studied at Yale and enlisted into the RFC in Canada in October 1917. In England he flew with a Home Defence squadron for a while before being sent to France to join No 40 Squadron. He saw all his action in the month of August 1918, in fact from the 15th to 24th, and in that brief period he shot down three German aircraft and nine kite balloons – actually on just six separate days. Balloons were very dangerous targets, always defended by any number of machine gun positions on the ground, and there was always the possibility of German air cover over the area of the balloon lines. Machine gun fire finally got Bennett on 24 August just after he had flamed his last two balloons and set his S.E.5 ablaze. Near the ground he was forced to jump from the burning aircraft and was severely injured, dying shortly afterwards. It was a double tragedy for his mother, who lost her husband on 16 August, although this news did not reach the son before he was killed in action.

33

Charles A Bissonette came from Los Angeles, born 27 December 1895. He joined the RFC in March 1917 and by the end of the year was in action with No 64 Squadron RFC. He claimed six victories before being rested in June 1918, then returned to fly with No 24 Squadron in September, but did not add to his score before the Armistice. He died in April 1971.

Sydney MacGillvary Brown hailed from Brooklyn, New York, born 10 August 1895. He joined the RFC after attending Princeton University and trained in Canada and England before going to No 29 Squadron on 4 July 1918! His DFC citation mentioned him as a fearless and intrepid pilot, and he accounted for four aircraft and a balloon to reach acedom. Brown died on 7 April 1952 in Pittsburgh.

Captain Alvin Andrew Callender, was born on Independence day – 4 July – in New Orleans, in 1893. Trained at Fort Worth and in England, he arrived at No 32 Squadron RFC on 15 May 1918. Gaining two victories he was then shot down himself but survived and by 24 September had scored eight victories. Becoming a flight commander he was shot down and killed in combat against Jasta 2 on 30 October.

From Fort Yates, North Dakota, where he was born 14 May 1897, John O Donaldson was sent to No 32 Squadron RAF for his combat experience. He remained to become not only an ace but a flight commander, winning the DFC and DSC for his seven Fokker D.VII victories during July and August 1918. However, his run was cut short on 1 September by being shot down by German ace Ltn Theodor Quandt of *Jasta 36,* the German's 11th of an eventual 15 victories. Taken prisoner he escaped the next day but was recaptured on the 9th, escaped again three days later and reached Holland the following month. Donaldson was killed in an air crash near Philadelphia on 7 September 1933.

John S Griffith, from Seattle, was born on 26 November 1898. He flew with No 60 Squadron from early 1918 and downed his 7th enemy aircraft on 7 July, which earned him the DFC. Hit by anti-aircraft fire 11 days later, his wounds put him out of the war, although he saw service with the White Russians against the Bolsheviks in Russia in 1919. During World War 2 he served with the US Army Air Corps. He died in October 1974.

Frank Lucien Hale was from Syracuse, NY, born 6 August 1895,

Charles A Bissonette shot down six German aircraft in the spring of 1918 flying S.E.5s with No 64 Squadron RAF. Here he is seen standing in front of a Sopwith Dolphin
(E F Cheesman)

Captain A A Callender, from New Orleans, downed eight German aircraft before falling in combat with *Jasta 2* fighters on 30 October 1918
(E F Cheesman)

John O Donaldson flew S.E.5s with No 32 Squadron shooting down seven Fokker D.VIIs in the summer of 1918 before becoming a prisoner on 1 September. He escaped twice, the second time successfully. The ribbon on his left breast is the initial version of the British DFC, which was later changed to the more familiar diagonal stripes
(E F Cheesman)

although he later lived in Arkansas. In 1914 he was back, joining 'D' Troop of the 4th Cavalry, New York National Guard, and then with the Ambulance Service he saw duty on the Mexican border in 1916. Rejected by the US Signal Corps (US aviation in the early days was no more than a section of the Signal Corps), 'Buddy' Hale successfully joined the RFC and became an ace with No 32 Squadron, claiming seven Fokker D.VIIs in the late summer of 1918. He also flew briefly with No 85 Squadron. He won the DFC and after the war served with the occupation forces in Germany.

Frank 'Buddy' Hale flew S.E.5s with No 32 Squadron, claiming seven victories over Fokker D.VIIs in the late summer of 1918
(E F Cheesman)

Before America came into World War 2 he joined the USAAC, and by 1943 was with the US 8th Air Force in England, but a heart condition forced his retirement. Working for the Bell Aircraft Corporation in Buffalo, New York, he died two months before his 50th birthday on 7 June 1944.

Duerson Knight, from Chicago, born 21 January 1893, served with No 1 Squadron RAF in 1918. 'Dewey' was involved in many combats during May and June and was credited with nine victories, many shared with other pilots. His 10th and final claim came on 22 August, a Fokker biplane brought down on the Allied side of the lines. He was then sent to an American squadron but did not see further combat. He died in California in June 1983.

Frank Hale and his S.E.5, E4026, of No 32 Squadron in 1918
(Franks collection)

Howard A Kullberg, from Somerville, Massachusetts, born 10 September 1896, attended Concord and Somerville schools, and finally Wentworth Institute in Boston. He joined the RFC in Toronto in August 1917 having been deemed too short to join the USAS. In May 1918 he was sent to No 1 Squadron and between then and September, claimed 19 combat victories, became a flight commander and won the DFC. His last victory came on 16 September but he was wounded also on this date, hit

three times in the leg by a Fokker D.VII. He saw out the war in hospital before returning home.

William Carpenter Lambert was another American to win the British DFC and run up a good score with the RAF. From Irontown, Ohio, where he was born on 18 August 1894, he had his first flight way back on 4 July 1910, during the Independence Day celebrations, being taken up in a Wright biplane, while still 15 years old. Working in Canada in 1915 he decided to join the RFC and in March 1918 was with No 24 Squadron. His 18 victories (his own unofficial list was 22) included two balloons. Invalided to England in August through combat fatigue, he lived until March 1982, a business man in his hometown. In World War 2 he served with the US Air Force and later rose to Lt-Colonel in the Reserve.

Jens F Larsen, from Waltham, Massachusetts, was born on 10 August 1891. Known inevitably as 'Swede', he joined the British army in Canada. Serving with the Field Artillery, he later transferred to the RFC in 1916. In July 1917 he went to the new No 84 Squadron and between November and April 1918 claimed nine victories, the last one being a two-seater he and three other pilots forced to crash inside Allied lines. After the war he became an architect.

No 40 Squadron in World War 1 was one of the more well known units in France. Alongside its many British aces was American Reed Gresham Landis who was born in Ottawa, Illinois, on 17 July 1896, the son of a judge. Before the war he lived in Chicago and in 1916 he became a member of the 1st Illinois Cavalry (National Guard) and saw service as a private on the Mexican border. In 1917 he joined the Aviation Section of the Signal Corps, completing his training in England prior to a posting to No 40 Squadron for operational experience. He acquired this in abundance, scoring 12 victories

Major Reed Landis, wearing his early DFC ribbon, won 12 victories between May and mid-August 1918 flying S.E.5s with No 40 Squadron. He ended the war commanding the 25th Pursuit Squadron (Bruce Robertson)

After notching up five victories during August and September 1918 flying S.E.5s with No 74 Squadron, Fred E. Luff transferred to the 25th Aero (E F Cheesman)

Francis Peabody Magoun, a Harvard graduate, was another American to fly S.E.5s and become an ace with No 1 Squadron RAF. After the war he returned to academic life (E F Cheesman)

Oren J Rose joined the RFC in 1917 and was the top-scoring pilot of No 92 Squadron, becoming flight commander and claiming 16 victories by the war's end (E F Cheesman)

between May and mid-August 1918, receiving the British DFC, and the DSC. He had flown alongside some notable Allied aces, among whom were Roderick Dallas and George McElroy. Fellow American Louis Bennett Jr was also with him. In August he was sent to command a flight in the US 25th Aero Squadron and the 4th Fighter Group, but the war ended before they could get into action. In the 1920s he became a member and later Chairman of the American Legion. During World War 2 Landis served in the USAAC as a colonel in Washington. He retired to Lake Ouachita, Arkansas, and died in 1975.

Frederick E Luff and H G Shoemaker also flew with a famous British squadron, No 74. From Cleveland, Ohio, Luff was born in 9 July 1896, eight days earlier than Reed Landis. Attached to the RAF for experience he gained five victories during August and September 1918 and was awarded the British DFC. In September he joined Landis in the 25th Aero. Back in America in 1919 he was injured in a crash at Lorain, Ohio, in May and never regained full health. He died at his parents' home in Cleveland in April 1931.

Harold G Shoemaker, known as 'Shoey', joined No 74 Squadron in early July 1918 and was credited with five victories by the end of August. Posted to the 17th Aero Squadron on 29 August, he had to change from an in-line engine to a rotary type, but he did not add to his score before he was killed in a mid-air collision with another American in his Camel over the German lines on 6 October.

New York is well represented by American aces, Frances Peabody Magoun being another from that city, born 6 January 1895. A graduate of Harvard he joined the US Ambulance Service, serving in France between March and August 1916. After a brief home stay, he returned to England to join the RFC and by November 1917 was with No 1 Squadron shortly before it got rid of its Nieuport Scouts and went over to the S.E.5. Magoun won the MC with this squadron but was wounded in

These S.E.5a's of No 85 Squadron were built under sub-contract and have had their serial numbers deleted by the censor. Elliott White Springs served in No 85 Squadron before going to the 148th Aero Squadron, as did Frank 'Buddy' Hale. Springs' aircraft is second from the bottom D6851 with an 'X' on the fuselage but a 'T' on the top wing *(Bruce Robertson)*

The inside of an S.E.5a cockpit. Note the control column complete with trigger mechanism. Ahead of the cockpit is a small, flat windscreen and the tube of the Aldis sight, with the fuselage-mounted Vickers gun to the left *(Bruce Robertson)*

A Fokker D.VII in factory finish lozenge-pattern printed fabric. Captured by the Allies in the closing stages of the war, it is a good example of the main fighter type facing the American Expeditionary Force in mid to late 1918
(Bruce Robertson)

April during a ground strafing sortie. He did not return until July but added one further victory to his score to become an ace, on 28 October. After the war he first became a graduate of Trinity College, Cambridge (England), and later a professor at Harvard. He died in Cambridge, Mass, on 5 June 1979.

Bogart Rogers was from Los Angeles, born 24 June 1898. After attending Stanford University, he joined the RFC in Canada in September 1917. By the early summer of 1918 he was flying with No 32 Squadron and his sixth victory went down under his guns on 1 November. He was then made a Captain. He lived until July 1966, passing away in Burbank, California.

Platte County, Missouri, was the home town of Oren J Rose, born 23 March 1893, who later lived in Kansas City. He joined the RFC in 1917 and went overseas in 1918. Once in France he was sent to No 92 Squadron and became this unit's highest scoring pilot with 16 victories by the war's end. He won the DFC and Bar and in 1919 served with the RAF in Russia. Post-war he went into the motor business in America and in World War 2 served in the USAAF as Operations and Training Officer in Kentucky. In 1943–44 he commanded a squadron in Louisiana and upon his release from duty in 1946 had become the Chief of the Aircraft Assignment Base at Wright Field, Dayton, Ohio. Returning to his car business he retired in the 1960s, living in Los Angeles, where he died in June 1971.

DOLPHIN ACES

On the Western Front in 1918 four RAF squadrons equipped with the Sopwith Dolphin, one of the rare Sopwith designs with an in-line engine as opposed to their usual rotary types. There was the usual smattering of Americans with these units too, and five became aces flying the Dolphin.

The most successful was Frederick W Gillet, born 28 November 1895 in Baltimore, Maryland. He went directly into the RFC in 1917 and by March the following year was posted to No 79 Squadron. He made slow progress and did not score until early August but then ran up an impressive 20 victories by the end of the war, his last three kills coming on 10 November, the day before the Armistice. The British awarded him the DFC and Bar, the Belgians their Croix de Guerre. The Squadron was occasionally asked to fly ground attack sorties and on one he was carrying small 25-lb bombs. Spotting a balloon on 1 September, he was about to attack but was inter-

The highest scoring pilot flying Sopwith Dolphins was Fred Gillet of No 79 Squadron. The last three of his 20 victories were achieved on 10 November 1918, the day before the Armistice (E F Cheesman)

rupted by the attentions of an LVG two-seater, probably a machine from one of the German *Schutzstaffeln* – ground attack units. He shot the two-seater down as the balloon was rapidly being hauled down, but Gillet dived down, dropped two bombs onto the winch crew, then fired into the gas-bag which was deflated but not flamed. Post-war Gillet went into a number of business ventures and died on 21 December 1969, aged 74.

In the same No 79 Squadron, Gillet had the company of another American, Frederick Ives Lord. Lord was another of those colourful characters that early flying seemed to produce. For one thing he was only 18 when he became a successful air ace, having lied about his age and produced a 'doctored' birth certificate. Born on 18 April 1900, he came from Manitowoc, Wisconsin, and had already seen service with the 3rd Texas Infantry before being found under age. Making his way to Canada his amended birth date got him into the RFC and by early 1918 he was in France flying Dolphins. Between the end of May and the end of September he accounted for 11 aircraft and one balloon, and received the

DFC and, despite his age, was a flight commander before being wounded in October.

In 1919 Lord flew against the Bolsheviks in Russia, but this time in an R.E.8 two-seater. He received a Bar to his DFC for attacking enemy columns from 200 feet which scattered men and horses, and blunted a planned assault on the White Russian forces. He also received two Russian decorations, one being the Order of St. Stanislaus 2nd Class with Swords. In the 1920s he became a 'barnstormer' in the US and began an air service between Texas and Mexico, and 1936 found him flying in the Spanish Civil War

Another colourful character flying Dolphins with No 79 Squadron was Fred I Lord. He downed 11 aircraft and a balloon despite being only 18 years old. After the war he flew an R.E.8 against the Bolsheviks in Russia and a Bréguet two-seater in the Spanish Civil War (E F Cheesman)

This well-known picture of No 1 Squadron on 3 July 1918 not only shows Knight (far left) and Kullberg too (in cockpit of C1835 far right) but also Knight's S.E.5 (C1106 'Y') in which he made three claims. Kullberg also made two claims in B8254 *(Franks collection)*

on the Republican side, flying Bréguet two-seaters. Early in World War 2 it was reported he joined the RAF again, using his old birth certificate and even got back to his old No 79 Squadron which was flying Hurricanes before officialdom caught up with him. Not to be out-done he started ferrying aircraft across the Atlantic to wartime Britain. He deserved a better fate, but in 1967 Fred Lord was murdered by a vagrant in California.

The other No 79 Squadron American ace was Edgar Taylor, from Central Falls, Long Island, New York. He arrived on this unit on 24 April 1918 but did not get his first combat victory – a Fokker D.VII – until 4 August. Before the month was out he had flamed four kite balloons, but in getting the final one on 24 August, he was hit and brought down by ground fire and did not survive.

James W Pearson and Harold A White were both aces with No 23 Squadron. Pearson came from Nutley, New Jersey, although he was born in Bridgeport, Connecticut, on 2 April 1895. When he arrived on No 23 Squadron they were still flying French SPADs, but soon after they re-equipped with Dolphins he began scoring victories. Between 30 May and the war's end he claimed 11 victories and received the DFC and the French Croix de Guerre with Palm. Back in New Jersey, he founded the J W Pearson Textile Company from which he retired in 1960. It was not until after his death in January 1993 that it was realised he was not only a World War 1 ace, but the only known surviving American ace of the Great War at that date.

Harry White was in Captain Jim Pearson's flight in No 23 Squadron. Sadly little is known of this ace, except that he claimed seven victories – all fighters – and won the DFC, gazetted in June 1919.

A NIEUPORT SCOUT ACE

While Americans with the *Lafayette* flew Nieuports, as did the early USAS pilots, only one American is known to have flown Nieuports with the British. D'Arcy Fowlis Hilton came from Michigan, although born in Toronto, Canada, on 17 October 1889, and later lived in Youngstown, New York. Sailing to England, he joined the RFC in November 1916 and became a pilot the following spring. In the early summer of 1917 he was sent to France and joined No 29 Squadron. By the late autumn he had claimed eight victories and been awarded the Military Cross. Back in England he became a flight instructor, and later moved to Canada where he continued in this role. For his good work he received the Air Force Cross. His marriage failed in 1924 and he appears to have slipped into obscurity. His son was killed flying on air operations in World War 2; Hilton himself died in October 1973.

Gillet's 79 Squadron Dophin, in which he claimed his last four victories *(Franks collection)*

Determined to become a pilot, D'Arcy Hilton sailed to England in 1916 and joined the RFC. Sent to France in the summer of 1917, he flew Nieuports with No 29 Squadron and achieved eight victories. He was the only American Nieuport Scout ace in the RFC *(E F Cheesman)*

THE SOPWITH CAMEL ACES

I n covering the American aces who flew Sopwith Camels, perhaps the most popular and well known of all World War 1 British fighter aircraft, we need to look at two distinct groups. Firstly, those who flew with British squadrons in both France and Italy, and those who flew with two American squadrons attached to the RAF.

WITH THE BRITISH

The most successful American Camel pilot with the British was Emile John Lussier, who, while often listed as a French-Canadian, was in fact born in Chicago, Illinois, on 10 October 1895 of a Canadian father. It was not until he was 15 years old that he went to Canada, his father taking a job in Winnipeg. By the time war came, Lussier was living in Alberta, and gave Medicine Hat as his home address. He enlisted into the RFC in late 1917, and after training, went to France and No 73 Squadron RAF. He won the DFC, the citation mentioning three enemy fighters shot down in one day, one in the morning, two in the afternoon, and nine of his claims were over Fokker D.VII biplanes. After the war he returned to America and became a farmer, but at the start of World War 2 Lussier immediately joined the Royal Canadian Air Force while the US was still neutral, and helped with wireless schools with the rank of squadron leader. After this war he returned to his American farm, and died after retirement, in Westminster, Maryland, in December 1974.

Another American who flew with No 73 Squadron in 1918 was Norman Cooper, whose real name had been E S Tooker. Originally a private in the 3rd Canadian Divisional Supply Column from June 1916 to August 1917, he then joined the RFC. His service and six victories brought him the British DFC and he ended the war as a Captain.

The next four Camel aces flew with former RNAS squadrons. Malcolm C Howell became an ace with No 208 Squadron in 1918 despite being injured at the start of his career on 15 May. However, on 28 July he shared the destruction of a Rumpler two-seater and gained his fifth victory on 5 October. Malcolm Clifford Howell was born 1 December 1895 and lived in 'Boonton', New Jersey. Leaving school he joined his father's real estate business in May 1917 but by July had volunteered for the RFC. Following his training he went to France in April 1918 and was posted to No 208 Squadron soon afterwards. However, he was injured in a crash on 15 May, but after recuperating returned to the squadron and by the war's end had claimed five victories – three fighters and two two-seaters. He died at Westchester, New York, in June 1976.

Emile J Lussier was the top-scoring American Camel pilot flying with the British. His aircraft carries the two white bars of No 73 Squadron RAF. Nine of his 11 victories were over Fokker D.VII biplanes
(E F Cheesman)

The other three Camel pilots served with No 210 Squadron, Messrs Pineau, Buchanan and Unger.

Cleo Francis Pineau came from Albuquerque, New Mexico, and was born on 23 July 1893. One of his pre-war loves was motor-cycle racing and no doubt speed dominated his thinking which is why he joined the RFC in Canada during December 1917. Completing his training in England he was sent to 210 and claimed his first victory on 6 September: a Fokker D.VII. His 6th and final claim came on 8 October, and it was his sixth Fokker biplane. However, on this same date he was shot down by a Fokker Triplane and became a prisoner of war. Having survived, he was awarded the DFC, and once released from PoW camp returned to the US. He died in Williamsport, Pennsylvania, in May 1972.

Archibald Buchanan was born on Long Island, New York, on 5 October 1892. He actually sailed to England to join the RNAS but by the time he became an operational pilot the RFC and RNAS had become the RAF. However, he distinguished himself during the summer of 1918, gaining seven victories, six fighters and a balloon, to win the DFC. On 17 October he landed at Ostend, Belgium, and was informed by the local inhabitants that he was the first Allied person to enter the town following the German retreat that morning. However, less than two weeks later, on the 30th, Archie Buchanan was shot down by a *Jasta 23* ace – Michael Hutterer – and spent the last 12 days of the war as a prisoner.

This prototype 2F Camel, developed for naval use, is fitted with the 130 hp (97 kW) Clerget rotary engine, and carries the atypical armament of a 0.303 in (7.7 mm) Vickers synchronised machine gun on the upper part of the forward fuselage and a Lewis machine gun on the centre section of the upper wing *(MARS)*

Pre-war motor cycle racer Cleo F Pineau shot down six Fokker D.VIIs in 1918 to become an ace, flying Camels with 210 Squadron RAF *(E F Cheesman)*

Kenneth R Unger, born 19 April 1898, came from Newark, New Jersey, but lived in Madison just prior to World War 1. Like a number of others, he was turned down by the USAS despite having learnt to fly and holding an American Aero (Flying) Certificate! Determined to fly, he travelled to Canada where he joined the RFC and once trained and in England, was sent to France to join No 210 Squadron on 11 June. In a massive air fight on 26 June, he and his flight commander and another pilot shared no fewer than four German fighters shot down (shared kills counted in a pilot's victory score in World War 1), and his fifth victory came on 20 July. Between then and the end of the war he ran up a further ten victory claims and won the DFC. Post-war Ken Unger flew with the US Air Mail Service, operating between Salt Lake City and Oakland, opened a training school and performed during air shows at Hadley airport. During one display in 1932 his machine broke up but he baled out successfully. During World War 2 he flew cargo 'planes for the US Navy, attaining the rank of Lt-Commander. He died in Florida, where he had retired in 1958, on 6 January 1979.

Ken Unger, another young pilot turned down by the USAS, served with No 210 Squadron. His aircraft carried the letter 'U' below the cockpit. By the end of the war, still only 20 years old, he had achieved 14 victories *(Franks collection)*

As well as American USAS pilots, there were a number of US Navy pilots operating in various capacities in England, France and Italy in 1918, and one of these became an ace flying with the RAF. David Sinton Ingalls from Cleveland, Ohio, born 28 January 1899, had attended Yale in late 1916 where he had joined its flying club. Reaching the age of 18 he was accepted into the US Navy as Naval Aviator No.85 and late 1917 found him attached to a RNAS squadron on the French Channel coast. He gained experience with No 13 Naval Squadron, then went to fly bombers with 17 Naval, which became No 217 Squadron RAF in April 1918. In August he returned to his former fighter unit, now No 213 Squadron, and began to score victories. His six claims that summer won him the British DFC, the DSC, the French Légion d'Honneur and a Mention in Despatches. He was the only US Navy ace in World War 1. He was in the legal profession after the war, but in World War 2 he was a ferry pilot and then a Navy Commander retiring as a Rear Admiral USNR, having seen duty in the Solomons in 1942. This war brought him a Bronze Star and the Legion of Merit. Post-World War 2 he became President of Pan American airlines and also went into publishing. In 1958 he returned to his law practice and died in Hunting Valley, Ohio, on 26 April 1985.

David S Ingalls, seen here in naval uniform, was the only US Navy ace in World War 1. Initially he was attached to a RNAS squadron based on the French Channel coast. He later claimed six victories flying Camels with No 213 Squadron RAF *(Franks collection)*

ITALY

Three British Camel squadrons were sent out to Italy at the end of 1917 to help combat the Austro-Hungarians fighting Britain's Italian ally in north-east Italy, Nos 28, 45 and 66. Two aces from these squadrons were Americans, H K Boyson and C G Catto.

Howard Koch Boyson, from Dallas, Texas, was born in 1892 and later lived in Chicago, Illinois. He volunteered for the RFC in June 1917 in Canada and after training was posted to No 66 Squadron while it was still flying Sopwith Pups. Once re-equipped with Camels he went to Italy with this unit and gained his first victory before 1917 was out. In May 1918 he added a further four scalps to his tally, and received the Italian Silver Medal for Military Valor.

Howard Boyson (left), a volunteer from Dallas, Texas, achieved five victories flying Camels with No 66 Squadron in Italy in 1918. With him is Alfred Koch MC, a Canadian ace with No 70 Squadron (*E F Cheesman*)

Charles G Catto was a medical student at Edinburgh when war broke out. He claimed his six victories flying Camels with No 45 Squadron over Italy before returning to Edinburgh to complete his studies (*Franks collection via Geo Williams*)

Charles Grey Catto also came from Dallas, Texas, born 7 November 1896. He was at Edinburgh University in Scotland studying medicine when war came, but when trying to enlist his parents objected. He continued his studies but eventually managed to join the RFC and was shipped out to Italy to join No 45 Squadron in March 1918. During the spring and summer of that year he claimed six victories, including one enemy two-seater Brandenburg forced to land inside Allied lines on 7 June. After the war he went on to complete his studies in Edinburgh and later became a doctor in his native Texas. He died on 24 June 1972.

THE AMERICAN CAMEL SQUADRONS

By early 1918 there were enough American pilots in service with the RAF to form two fighter squadrons. Those posted to either had two trains of thought: on the one hand they were all Americans together, on the other, they were all inexperienced and going to an experienced front-line outfit might provide better survival rates. Nevertheless, those posted to either the 17th or 148th Squadrons had little choice but to get on with it.

17TH AERO

The 17th Pursuit Squadron was formed in the US in 1917. Sent to France, it began operating in July 1918, as part of the British 65th Wing. It

Howard Burdick (top), from Brooklyn, with eight victories was the highest scoring ace with the 17th Aero Squadron. Francis M Simonds Jr (below) made ace with the 147th Aero. Both were members of the Toronto Group of aviators. *(Franks collection)*

Howard C Knotts flew Camels with the 17th Aero for his six confirmed victories, to which he added seven more by burning a train which was transporting Fokkers, a daring deed carried out whilst he was a prisoner of war *(Bruce Robertson)*

George A Vaughn Jr flew Camels with the 17th Aero after flying S.E.5s with No 84 Squadron RAF. He became an ace with both units totting up 13 victories *(Bruce Robertson)*

produced several aces, the highest scoring of whom was Howard Burdick from Brooklyn, New York. Born 12 December 1891, Burdick received the DFC for eight victories scored during September and October, all deemed destroyed – four Fokker biplanes and four two-seaters. His son Clinton D Burdick became an ace in World War 2 flying Mustangs with the 8th Air Force in England. Howard Burdick died in Los Angeles in January 1975.

Howard Clayton Knotts came from Carlinsville, Illinois, having been born in Girard on 25 August 1895. He joined the USAS and trained in Canada. One victory in August 1918 and five during September made him an ace. He received both the British DFC and the American Distinguished Service Cross. On 14 October he was shot down and taken prisoner but during his train journey to prison camp he spotted some enemy aircraft being shipped by rail to the front. Somehow he managed to start a fire which destroyed seven Fokker biplanes. He was almost shot by firing squad but survived. After the war he entered the legal profession becoming a noted aviation lawyer. He died from a heart attack on 23 November 1942, aged 47.

George A Vaughn Jr might have been covered in the S.E.5 section of this book, as he had already attained seven victories flying this type with the British No 84 Squadron during June through August 1918. Another from Brooklyn, New York, George was born on 20 May 1897 and was a graduate of Princeton, where he joined the University's Aero Club in 1917. Joining the USAS he came to England and after a period ferrying aircraft to France, was posted to No 84 Squadron. Of his seven victories with this unit, six were deemed destroyed, one out of control. On 27 August he was transferred to the 17th as a flight commander, adding a further six victories to his score despite the complete change of aircraft, from the in-line engined S.E.5 to the rotary engined Camel. After the war he remained interested in aviation, became an aeronautical engineer and a partner in the Casey Jones Academy of Aeronautics at La Guardia Airport in New York. He died from a brain tumour on Staten Island, on the last day of July 1989.

Another American to gain acedom in two British units was Lloyd A Hamilton, from Troy, New York, born on 13 June 1894. After completing his education at Syracuse University in 1916 he entered

Harvard, and as America entered the war he enlisted into Aviation. Coming to England in the autumn of 1917 he was assigned to No 3 Sqn in March 1918 and between 11 April and 3 June accounted for five enemy aircraft. Hamilton was then posted to the 17th Aero to help complete their training, then became a flight commander upon going to the front. During August he downed a further three German aircraft and two balloons to bring his score to ten. He won the British DFC and American DSC, both citations recording his daring attack on Varssenaere airfield, Belgium, on 13 August, destroying, with his flight, aircraft and hangars and shooting-up a nearby château which housed German officers causing many casualties. He was finally brought down by ground fire on 24 August and crashed to his death.

Lloyd A Hamilton gained acedom with two squadrons, No 3 RAF, and the 17th Aero. He carried out a devastating raid on Varssenaere airfield, Belgium, on 12 August 1918 but was killed in action twelve days later *(E F Cheesman)*

Robert M Todd became an ace with the 17th during August 1918. From Cincinnati, Ohio, born 24 June 1897, Bob Todd was an engineering student at the local university and joined the USAS in August 1917, then graduated from the Ohio State University of Aeronautics that October. Flying with the 17th in France his fifth victory was claimed on 26 August, when he was shot down in a massive action with *Jasta 2* and *Jasta 27*. Seven of the Squadron's Camels were shot down, Todd being injured and taken prisoner – thought to have been shot down by Ltn Rudolf Klimke of *Jasta 27*, the German's 13th of an eventual 16 victories. After the war Todd went into engineering and served in the USAAC during World War 2 in both the US and England. In 1982 he finally received a Purple Heart, 64 years after his injuries from 26 August 1918. He died in La Jolla, California, 20 January 1988.

William D Tipton, from Jarrettsville, Maryland, became an ace with the 17th. Born 11 December 1892, Bill Tipton joined the USAS and was sent

In 1918 Bob Todd scored five victories flying Camels with the 17th Aero, but was shot down and taken prisoner before he could do any more damage *(Franks collection)*

to France in early 1918 to gain experience with the British. He was assigned, like Hamilton, to No 3 Squadron on 12 March and in May 1918 shot down two German two-seater aircraft. He was transferred to the 17th, on 21 June and later commanded B Flight. 'Tip' added a balloon and two Fokker biplanes to his tally during August but, like Bob Todd, was brought down in combat on 26 August to become a prisoner. After the war he was awarded the DFC. Also like Todd, Bill Tipton served again in World War 2, with the USAAC, reaching the rank of

William D Tipton of the 17th Aero had just made ace when he was shot down and taken prisoner on 26 August 1918 *(Franks collection)*

One of the most colourful and famous American pilots of the Great War was Elliott White Springs from South Carolina. His first kill was a Pfalz D III on 1 June 1918 while flying with No 85 Squadron RAF. By the end of the month his score had risen to four. In July he transferred to the all-American 148th Aero, ending the war as a 16-victory ace. Below he stands beside his British marked Sopwith Camel, while on the right he appears to have survived a slight mishap *(US National Archives)*

Colonel, but was killed in a flying accident piloting a P47 Thunderbolt at Odema, Ohio, on 12 December 1945.

148TH AERO

This unit was formed at Kelly Field, Texas, in late 1917. Once in France and under RAF control in July 1918 it produced five aces, and had two other pilots who became aces. By far the most colourful and famous pilot in the 148th was Elliott White Springs.

Born in Fort Hill, South Carolina, on 31 July 1896 he later lived in Lancaster. Educated at Culver Military Academy and Princeton University, he trained as an aviation cadet in late 1917 and was sent to England to gain operational experience with the British. His first posting was to No 85 Squadron, flying S.E.5s, and in June 1918 he scored four victories with this unit before being sent to the newly formed 148th Pursuit. As a flight commander he accounted for a further 12 hostile aircraft – ten being Fokker biplanes – which brought him the DFC and DSC. Late in the war he became the 148th's CO as both it and the 17th joined the US 4th Pursuit Group, but this outfit did not have time to get into action by the war's end. After the war he flew some 'barnstorming' flights in the US and wrote several books, the most famous of which was *War Birds*, based on the diary of John McG Grider, a fellow American who was killed flying with No 85 Squadron with Springs. He later became Vice-President of his father's cotton mills – and later a multi-millionaire – until 1941, at which time he served in the USAAC. He died of cancer in a New York hospital on 15 October 1959.

Field Eugene Kindley, born Pea Ridge, Arkansas, on 13 March 1896, came from farming stock.

All but one of Field Kindley's 12 victories were scored flying Camels with the 148th Aero. He was killed in a flying accident in February 1919 *(E F Cheesman)*

However, he became a motion picture operator before enlisting into the Kansas National Guard in May 1917, then transferred into aviation. By the time he was a qualified pilot he was sent to No 65 Squadron RAF to fly Camels with the British and scored one victory on 26 June 1918. Assigned to the 148th he shot down a further ten aircraft and a balloon, making a total score of 12. He received the DFC and DSC with Oak Leaf Cluster, and after the war became CO of the 94th Pursuit at Kelly Field, San Antonio, Texas. On 1 February 1920 he was killed in a flying accident. Hamilton Air Force Base on Bermuda was renamed Kindley Field in his memory.

Henry Robinson Clay Jr made ace with the 148th. Born Plattsburg, Missouri, on 27 November 1895, he later lived in Fort Worth, Texas. Hank Clay went to England with the USAS trainees and gained combat experience with No 43 Squadron RAF in May 1918 where he had one unconfirmed victory before going to the 148th. In August and September he downed eight German aircraft, won the DFC and DSC, and was then given command of the 41st Aero, but the war ended before this unit saw action. Clay was a victim of the massive influenza epidemic that swept the world towards the end of World War 1, and he died in Coblenz, Germany, on 17 February 1919.

Henry R Clay Jr, seen standing by a Camel, downed eight German aircraft with the 148th Aero. He survived the war but died in the influenza epidemic in February 1919 *(E F Cheesman)*

Jesse Orin Creech was born in Harlin, Kentucky, on 22 August 1896, and lived in Washington DC pre-war. Going through the USAS system he was posted to the 148th in the summer of 1918 and won the DFC for shooting down seven German aircraft. Surviving the war he lived until 16 February 1948, dying in Louisville, Kentucky.

Jesse O Creech, from Washington DC, gained seven victories flying Camels with the 148th Aero *(E F Cheesman)*

Clayton L Bissell was an ace with the 148th. From Kane, Pennsylvania. Clay was born in 29 July 1896 and obtained a law degree from the Valparaiso University of Indiana. He then joined the USAS and flying with the 148th won the British DFC and American DSC for his six victories scored between August and October 1918. In 1919 he commanded the 639th Aero in occupied Germany and remained in the Air Force, rising to the rank of Major-General. In the 1920s he flew with Billy Mitchell and was on the

famous flight which bombed and sank the *Ostrieland*, proving Mitchell's air power theories. During World War 2 he served mainly in China and later commanded the US 10th Air Force in India. Later still he became Chief of Intelligence, and post-World War 2 was air attaché in London

Lt Thomas L Galbreath of Philadelphia, Pa, who flew Camels with the 148th Aero in pukka flying clothing *(Phil Jarrett)*

Clayton L Bissell of the 148th Aero, securely wrapped in a sensible scarf, achieved six victories in 1918. He enjoyed a distinguished post-war career in the US Air Force until his retirement in 1950 *(Franks collection)*

Orville Ralston had gained three victories flying S.E.5s with No 85 Squadron RAF, before transferring to the 148th where he brought his score up to five (E F Cheesman)

Lawrence Callahan and Camel. Callahan added two victories flying Camels with the 148th to add to his three kills with No 85 Squadron RAF (E F Cheesman)

F.I Camels of 148th Aero lined up at Petit Synthe on 6 August 1918. The nearest aircraft, D9516, was lost on 28 August and its pilot, Lt G V Siebold, killed in action (Phil Jarrett)

1946-48. He retired from the service in 1950 and died on 24 September 1972 in Murfreesboro, Tennessee.

The two pilots who became aces with the 148th were A O Ralston and L K Callahan. Orville A Ralston, from Lincoln, Nebraska – born 19 November 1897 – joined the USAS and flew S.E.5s with No 85 Squadron, gaining two victories, before assigned to the 148th. With this unit he downed three more to become an ace. He died in May 1970.

Lawrence K Callahan, from Louisville, Kentucky, was born 11 January 1894 and was a graduate of Cornell College. Living in Chicago, he joined the USAS and trained with the RFC in England. He too went to No 85 Squadron in 1918, claimed three victories flying the S.E.5, and then with the 148th made ace on 28 October with his second kill of that month, and won the British DFC. During World War 2 he served with the USAAC, part of his duty taking him to serve with the 12th US Air Force in Oran, Algeria. He died on 17 September 1977 in Gardena, California.

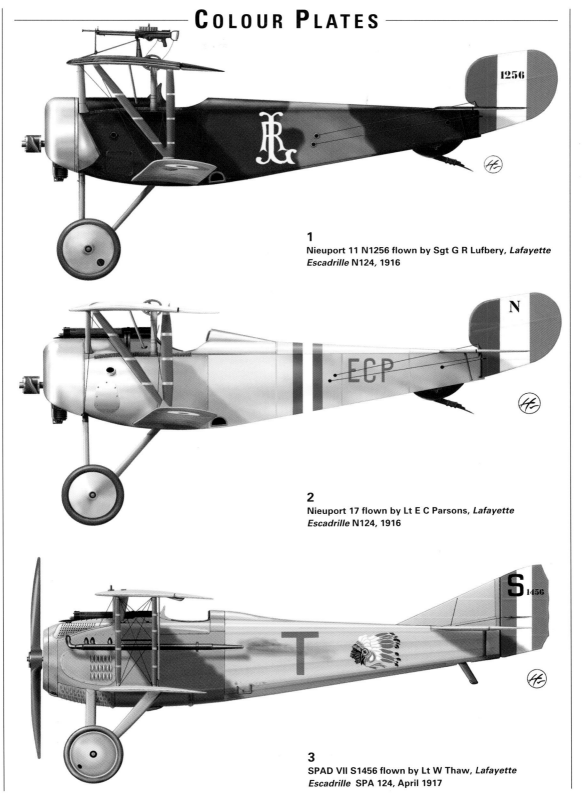

1
Nieuport 11 N1256 flown by Sgt G R Lufbery, *Lafayette Escadrille* N124, 1916

2
Nieuport 17 flown by Lt E C Parsons, *Lafayette Escadrille* N124, 1916

3
SPAD VII S1456 flown by Lt W Thaw, *Lafayette Escadrille* SPA 124, April 1917

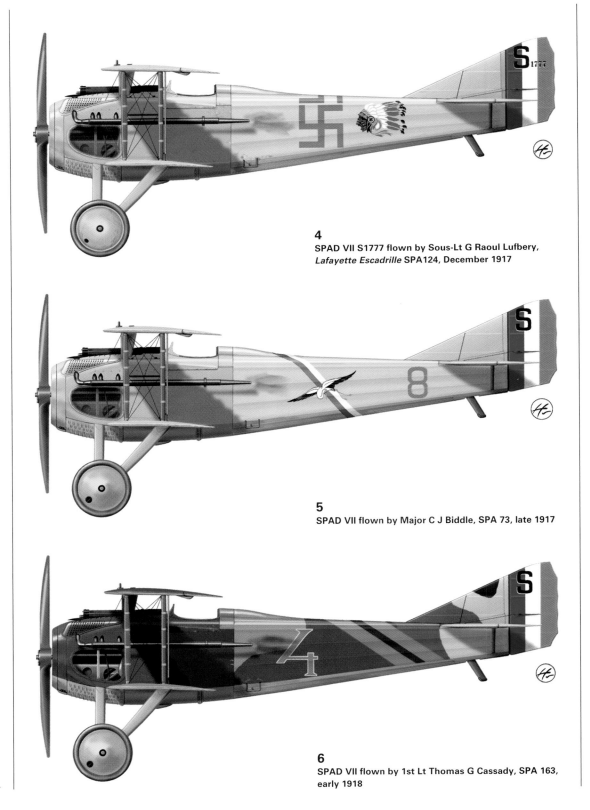

4
SPAD VII S1777 flown by Sous-Lt G Raoul Lufbery,
Lafayette Escadrille SPA124, December 1917

5
SPAD VII flown by Major C J Biddle, SPA 73, late 1917

6
SPAD VII flown by 1st Lt Thomas G Cassady, SPA 163,
early 1918

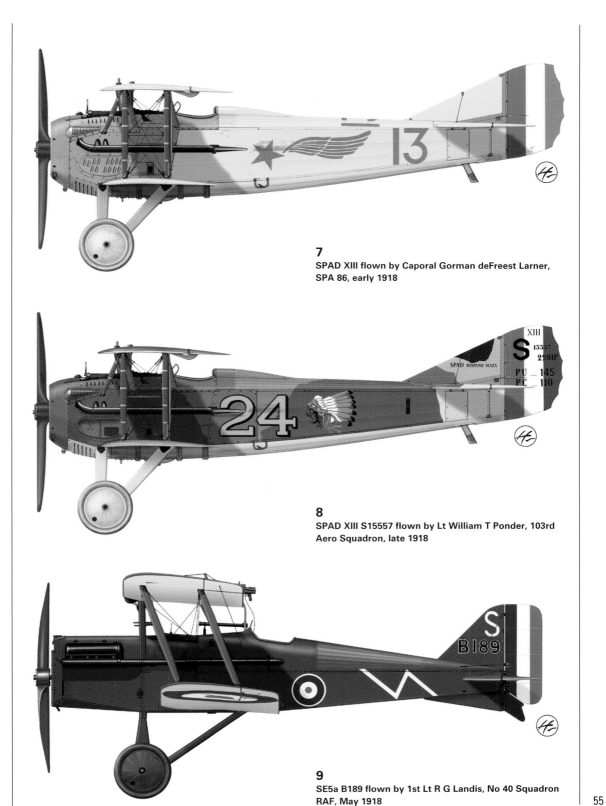

7
SPAD XIII flown by Caporal Gorman deFreest Larner,
SPA 86, early 1918

8
SPAD XIII S15557 flown by Lt William T Ponder, 103rd
Aero Squadron, late 1918

9
SE5a B189 flown by 1st Lt R G Landis, No 40 Squadron
RAF, May 1918

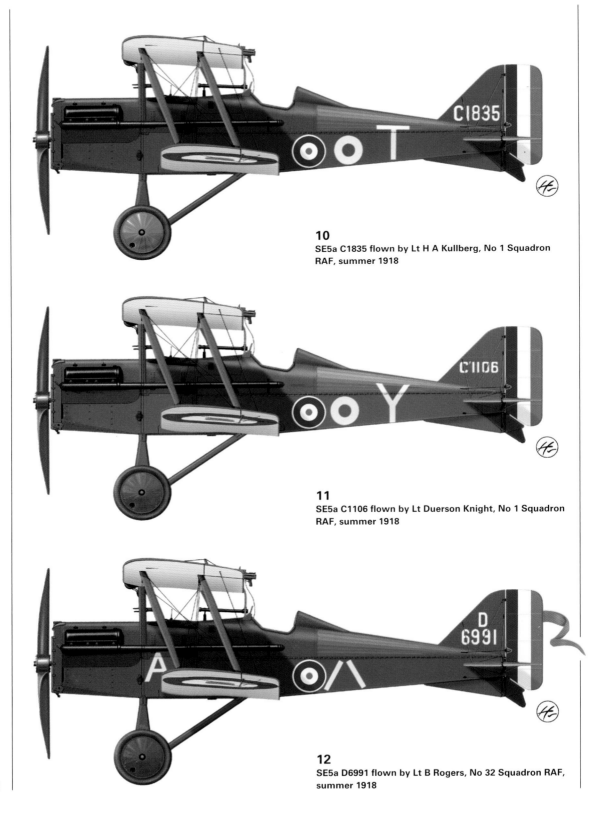

10
SE5a C1835 flown by Lt H A Kullberg, No 1 Squadron
RAF, summer 1918

11
SE5a C1106 flown by Lt Duerson Knight, No 1 Squadron
RAF, summer 1918

12
SE5a D6991 flown by Lt B Rogers, No 32 Squadron RAF,
summer 1918

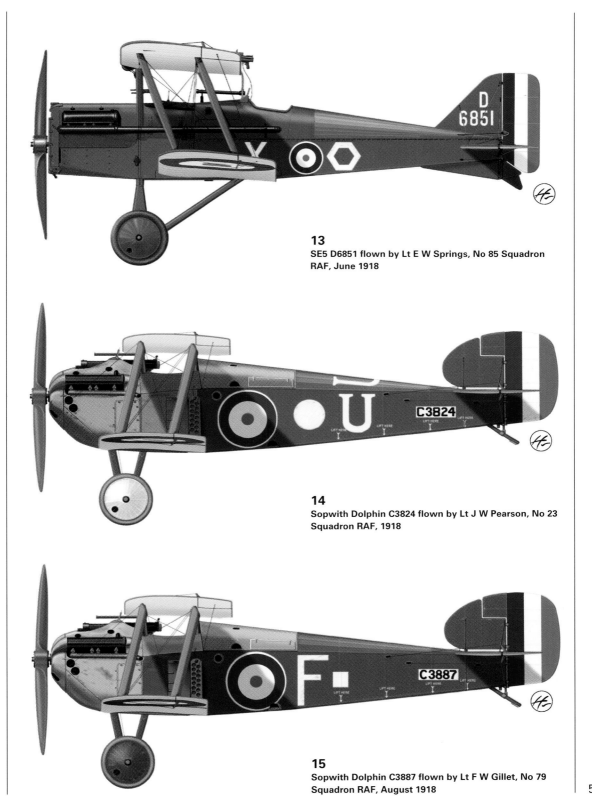

13
SE5 D6851 flown by Lt E W Springs, No 85 Squadron
RAF, June 1918

14
Sopwith Dolphin C3824 flown by Lt J W Pearson, No 23
Squadron RAF, 1918

15
Sopwith Dolphin C3887 flown by Lt F W Gillet, No 79
Squadron RAF, August 1918

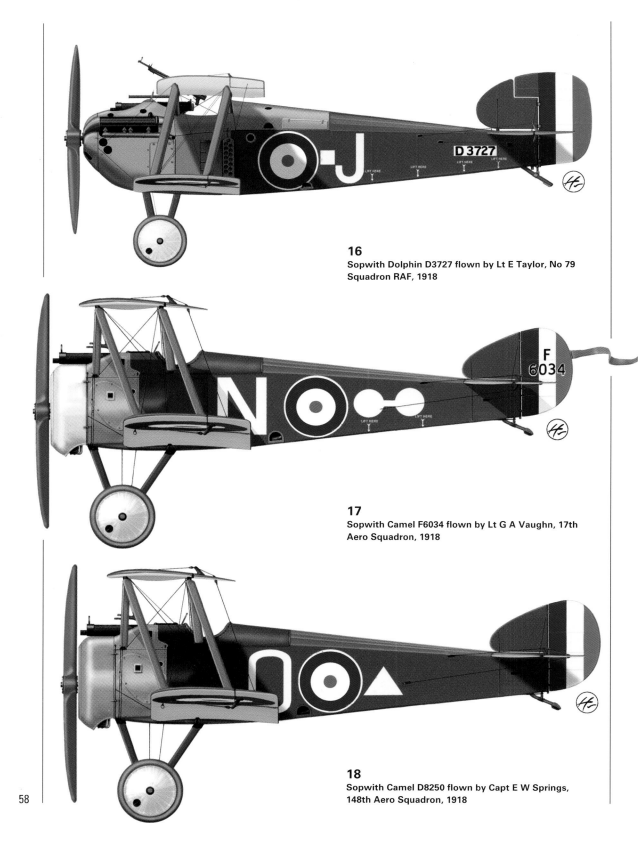

16
Sopwith Dolphin D3727 flown by Lt E Taylor, No 79
Squadron RAF, 1918

17
Sopwith Camel F6034 flown by Lt G A Vaughn, 17th
Aero Squadron, 1918

18
Sopwith Camel D8250 flown by Capt E W Springs,
148th Aero Squadron, 1918

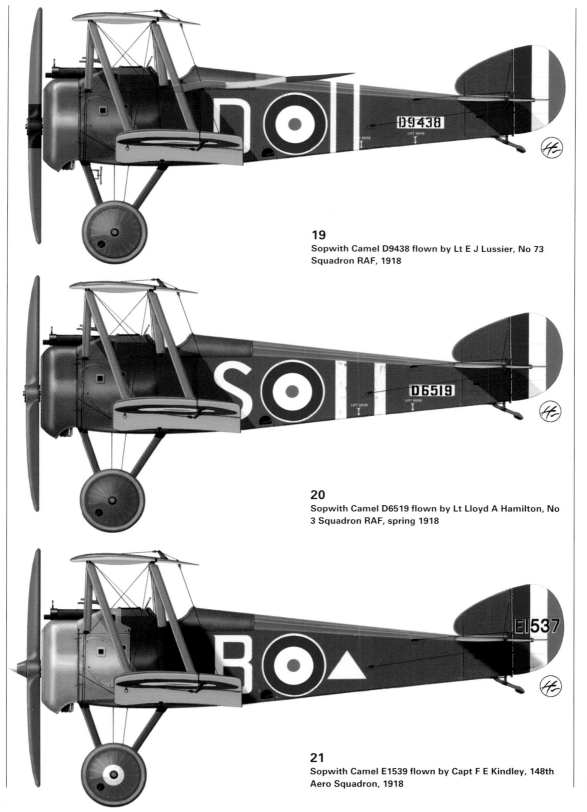

19
Sopwith Camel D9438 flown by Lt E J Lussier, No 73
Squadron RAF, 1918

20
Sopwith Camel D6519 flown by Lt Lloyd A Hamilton, No
3 Squadron RAF, spring 1918

21
Sopwith Camel E1539 flown by Capt F E Kindley, 148th
Aero Squadron, 1918

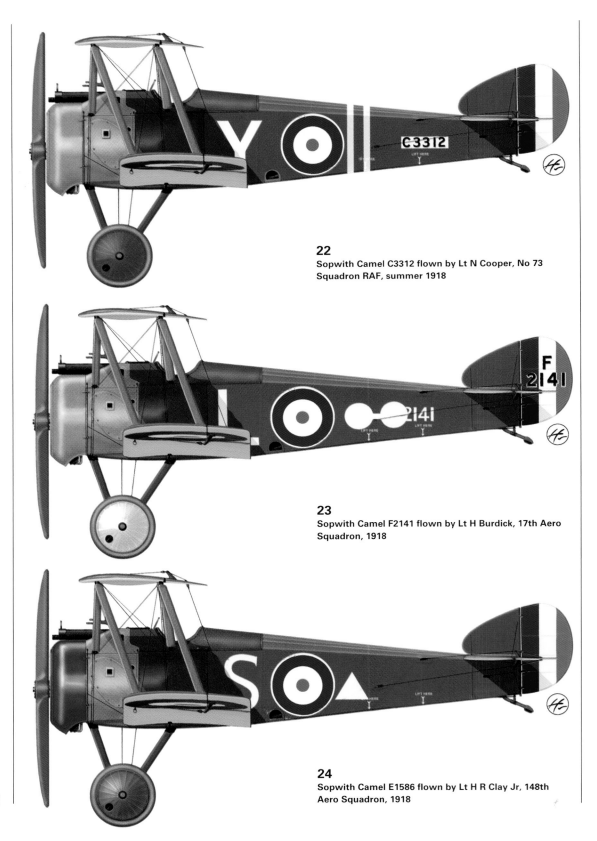

22
Sopwith Camel C3312 flown by Lt N Cooper, No 73
Squadron RAF, summer 1918

23
Sopwith Camel F2141 flown by Lt H Burdick, 17th Aero
Squadron, 1918

24
Sopwith Camel E1586 flown by Lt H R Clay Jr, 148th
Aero Squadron, 1918

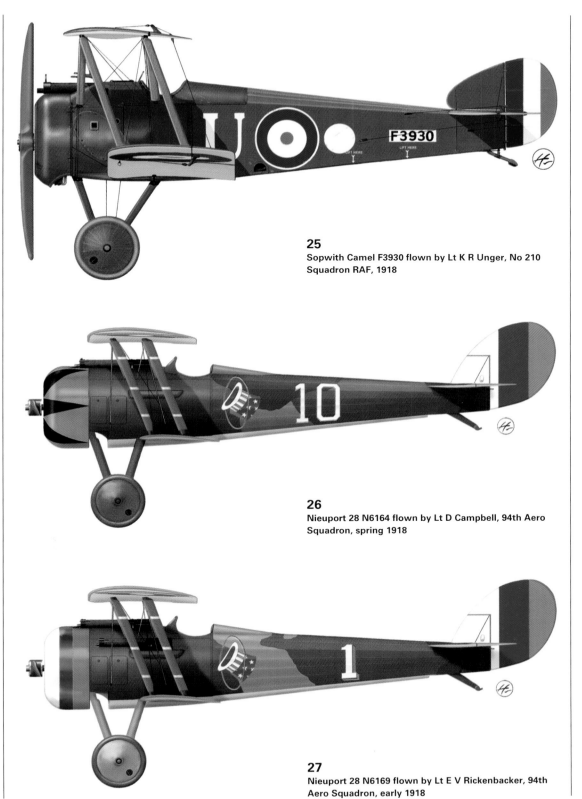

25
Sopwith Camel F3930 flown by Lt K R Unger, No 210
Squadron RAF, 1918

26
Nieuport 28 N6164 flown by Lt D Campbell, 94th Aero
Squadron, spring 1918

27
Nieuport 28 N6169 flown by Lt E V Rickenbacker, 94th
Aero Squadron, early 1918

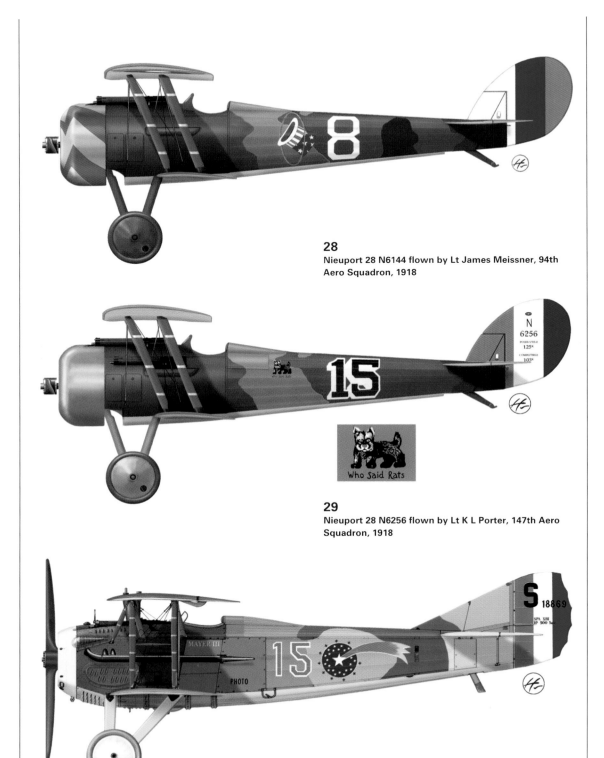

28
Nieuport 28 N6144 flown by Lt James Meissner, 94th
Aero Squadron, 1918

29
Nieuport 28 N6256 flown by Lt K L Porter, 147th Aero
Squadron, 1918

30
SPAD XIII S18869 flown by Capt J M Swaab, 22nd Aero
Squadron, 1918

31
SPAD XIII S4489 flown by Capt C J Biddle, 13th Aero
Squadron, 1918

32
SPAD XIII S4523 flown by Capt E V Rickenbacker, 94th
Aero Squadron, 1918

33
SPAD XIII S15202 flown by Lt F Luke Jr, 27th Aero
Squadron, September 1918

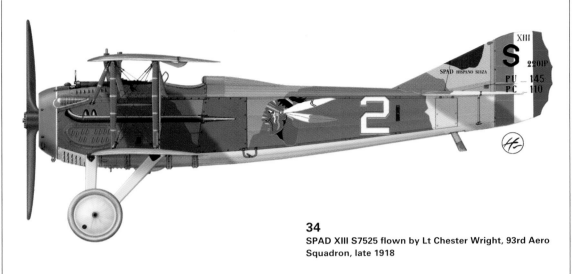

34
SPAD XIII S7525 flown by Lt Chester Wright, 93rd Aero
Squadron, late 1918

35
SPAD XIII S15034 flown by Lt Hamilton Coolidge, 94th
Aero Squadron, late 1918

VIRGINIA-ANN

36
SPAD XIII S15191 'VIRGINIA-ANN' flown by 1st Lt Karl
Schoen, 139th Aero Squadron, 1918

AMERICAN ACES IN THE US AIR SERVICE

With no front-line aircraft of its own, the USAS became dependent on aircraft from both France and Britain in order for its war pilots to fight on the side of the Allies. On the fighter side, Americans could and did fly a variety of machines with the British and French, but advanced units of the USAS in France were equipped solely with the Nieuport 28.

It may seem strange that this French fighter did not see action with its own air force, obviously French pilots found that the SPAD XIII, which had already started to replace the successful SPAD VII, was a first-rate machine, so this new Nieuport 28 design was available in numbers for the Americans. Among the first American units to arrive in France was the 95th Pursuit during November 1917, followed by the 94th, activated in France in March 1918. During this period the *Lafayette Escadrille* became the 103rd Aero. Other squadrons quickly followed as the year progressed.

The first Nieuports to arrive for the 94th and 95th did not carry guns, but despite this several cautious patrols were flown along the front for experience. Once the guns arrived, the USAS's air war began. These units were then formed into the American 1st Pursuit Group.

—— 1st Pursuit Group USAS ——

Once the USAS began to be established in France, the fighter squadrons were gradually formed into Groups. The 1st Pursuit Group would eventually comprise the 94th, 95th, 27th and 147th Squadrons. The Group was under the command of Lieutenant-Commander Bert M Atkinson.

Douglas Campbell was the first US trained pilot to become an ace. Flying with the 94th Aero he claimed six victories in the spring of 1918 before being wounded. Here he stands by a Nieuport 28 carrying the famous hat-in-ring insignia of the 94th *(E F Cheesman)*

Eddie Rickenbacker, one-time chauffeur to General Pershing, became the American ace of aces with 26 victories and received a belated Medal of Honor to add to his DSC and 9 Oak Leaf Clusters, Légion d'Honneur and Croix de Guerre. Here he poses by the wheel of the SPAD XIII he flew with 94th Aero Squadron *(via Bruce Robertson)*

Douglas Campbell made history as the first American trained ace flying with the 94th in the spring of 1918. From San Jose, near San Francisco, Campbell was born on 7 June 1896 and attended Harvard whilst living in Mt. Hamilton. Then at Cornell he began aviation training which was completed in France before being assigned to the 94th in January 1918 and he gained his first victory on 14 April. His two Pfalz Scouts and four Rumpler two-seater victories won for him the DSC with four Oak Leaf Clusters, the French Légion d'Honneur and the Croix de Guerre with two palms. Wounded on 5 June he returned to the US, not returning to France until after the war's end. In 1935 he was with Pan American Airways later becoming a vice-president in 1939 and General Manager in 1948. Retiring to Cos Cob, Connecticut, in 1963 he died in Greenwich, Conn., on 16 December 1990.

David Peterson (mentioned in Chapter One) became an ace with the 94th after flying with the French, but Edward Vernon Rickenbacker became an ace by the end of May 1918. 'Rick' also became the American 'ace of aces' with 26 victories, although it took till 1960 to get confirmation of one victory. It also took 12 years for his country to award him the Medal of Honor – only the second US World War 1 fighter pilot so honoured.

Rickenbacker was born in Columbus, Ohio, on 8 October 1890 and his early life was combined with speed – motor racing. In 1916 he went to England with the car industry, got caught up with the war fever and once America came into the conflict, he became a driver on General John J Pershing's staff. He managed to transfer into Aviation and by early 1918 was with the 94th. Between April and May he downed six German machines but then an ear infection took him away from the front until the late summer. Returning to the 94th he ran up a score of 25 plus that one unconfirmed by the end of October. He was awarded the DSC with nine

Oak Leaf Clusters, the French Croix de Guerre with three palms and finally the Légion d'Honneur. After the war he returned to the motor business and civil aviation, setting up his own business and an airline. In World War 2 he went on many tours to meet men in front-line duty and in 1942 was lucky to survive a crash in the Pacific, resulting in three weeks on a raft. He died on 27 July 1973 in Zurich, Switzerland.

Hamilton Coolidge flew SPAD XIIIs with the 94th Aero in 1918. He had scored eight victories before his death in combat on 27 October (*Bruce Robertson*)

As 1918 progressed the 94th produced further aces. Hamilton Coolidge from Brookline, Mass., born 1 September 1895, began flying after Harvard and entered the Air Service in March 1917. Working in Paris on the organisation side he did not complete his flight training until later but eventually went to the front. He shot down five aircraft and three balloons but was killed in action on 27 October 1918. His DSC came through after the war, which was added to his French Croix de Guerre and palm. He also had four unconfirmed victories.

Reed McKinley Chambers, from Memphis, Tennessee, born 18 August 1894 in Onaga, Kansas, joined the Tennessee National Guard in 1914 seeing duty on the Mexican border in 1916. Joining the Air Service he was assigned to the 94th and by the end of the war had achieved seven confirmed victories, including one balloon. He received the DSC and three Clusters, and the Légion d'Honneur and the Croix de Guerre with two palms, one silver and one bronze star. Post-war he flew as a test

Captains E R Cook and R McK Chambers in front of a captured Fokker D.VII. Reed Chambers became an ace with the 94th Aero with seven victories, while Everett Cook gained five victories with his observers flying with the 91st Observation Squadron in late 1918 (*Bruce Robertson*)

pilot, helped run an airline with Eddie Rickenbacker, then formed an aviation insurance group. In 1968 he flew second pilot in a F-106 jet and went through the sound barrier. He died at St Thomas in the Virgin Islands, on 16 January 1972.

Another seven-victory ace with the 94th was Harvey Weir Cook who was from Wilkenson, Indiana, but also lived in Ohio pre-war. He was with the 94th for the final months of World War 1 claiming three aircraft and four balloon kills, which won for him the DSC with one Oak Leaf Cluster. In World War 2 he served in the Air Corps but was killed flying a P-40 fighter in New Zealand on 25 March 1943, aged 50.

Assigned to the 94th in March 1918 was James A Meissner, from Brooklyn, New York, although he was born in Nova Scotia on 20 July 1896. Graduating from Cornell University, Jimmy Meissner enlisted into the Aviation Service in 1917. In France he gained his first victory on 2 May 1918 but was lucky to survive the encounter as the fabric of his top wing ripped away. He was awarded the DSC and went on to score four kills with the 94th – one by collision, which brought him a second DSC – before going to command the 147th Aero where he shot down four more. Post-war he helped form the Alabama National Guard, which he later commanded. He died on 16 January 1936.

During July 1918 the 94th and 95th began replacing their Nieuports with SPAD XIIIs and the two new units within the Group (1st Pursuit Group), the 27th and 147th also began to change equipment.

With the 95th, two pilots gained seven victories. First was Sumner Sewell from Bath, Maine, born 17 June 1897, and a graduate of Harvard. Initially with the US Ambulance Service in France between February and August 1917 he enlisted in the USAS in Paris and after training went to the 95th in February 1918. He eventually made flight commander but did not open his account until 3 June. On

James A Meissner first flew with the 94th and later commanded the 147th Aero. At the time of his first victory he had a lucky escape as the fabric of the top wing of his 28 was ripped off. Undeterred he went on to gain seven more victories. His portrait shows his DSC and Cluster, *Croix de Guerre* and two palms and above his wings, the badge of the 94th Squadron. *(Bruce Robertson)*

The Fokker D.VII 4635/18 flown by Lt Heinz Freiherr von Beaulieu-Marconnay of *Jasta 65* was captured by three pilots of the 95th Aero Squadron, one of whom was Sumner Sewell. Its pilot had landed in fog on the 95th's airfield and the three pilots had taken the German prisoner at gunpoint *(Bruce Robertson)*

5 November he gained his 7th victory, one of two balloons flamed on successive days to add to his five aircraft victories. With two DSCs and the Croix de Guerre, the Belgian Order of Léopold and Aero Club of America Medal, he returned home in 1919. One 'victory' not listed was a Fokker D.VII whose pilot became lost and landed at the 95th's airfield. Sewell was among the men who took the pilot captive before he could take off again. Sewell went into politics, becoming a State Senator in the '30s, then Governor of Maine between 1941 and 1945. Made President of the Bath National Bank in the 1960s, he died in his home town on 26 January 1965.

Lancing C Holden Jr from New York, born on 8 October 1896, became a graduate of Princeton, where he joined the flying group. Going to France he was attached to the French N 471 *Escadrille* between April and July 1918. With the 95th he gained two aircraft and five balloon victories to win the DSC and Oak Leaf Cluster, even surviving a shoot-down on 10 August. Completing his studies at Princeton post-war he became an architect like his father. Back in France in 1924, he married and the following year 'Denny', as he'd become known, served with other Americans in Morocco against the Riffian uprising with the rank of captain. For his service he received the Légion d'Honneur and the

Sumner Sewell shot down five aircraft and two balloons with the 95th Aero. After the war he had a successful career in politics, becoming a state senator and Governor of Maine during the years of World War 2 *(Bruce Robertson)*

Lancing C Holden Jr (on left) initially flew with the French *Escadrille* N 471. He later shot down five balloons and two aircraft with the 95th Aero. On the right is Zenos Miller of the 27th Aero who became an ace the day he was brought down and made prisoner, 20 July. Note the 27th Aero's eagle pin above Miller's right pocket *(Franks collection)*

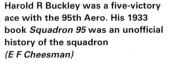

Ed Curtis joined the USAS in 1917 and became a six-victory ace with the 95th. He rose to Major General in the USAAF in World War 2 *(Franks collection via C Woolley)*

Harold R Buckley was a five-victory ace with the 95th Aero. His 1933 book *Squadron 95* was an unofficial history of the squadron *(E F Cheesman)*

Croix de Guerre. In 1932 he went to Hollywood briefly to help with motion pictures before returning to New York. He was an officer with the National Guard and flying with the 102nd Observation Squadron, was killed in an air crash near Sparta, Tennessee, on 13 November 1938 in bad weather.

Rochester, New York, saw the birth of Edward P Curtis on 14 January 1897. He joined the USAS in 1917 and in February he was with the 95th in France. He was with this unit for the whole of 1918, gaining six victories, and won the DSC. After the war he worked for the Eastman Kodak Company in New York and in World War 2 became a Major-General in the USAAF. He died in his home town, on 13 March 1987.

Unofficial historian of the 95th through his book *Squadron 95* was Harold R Buckley, from Westfield, Mass., born 4 April 1896. Another entrant via the Ambulance Service, Buckley joined the USAS in Paris and found himself with the 95th in March 1918. Four aircraft and one balloon made him an ace and the recipient of a DSC and Oak Leaf, the Croix de Guerre and a Medal from the Aero Club of America. Post-war he lived in Paris for a time, and and wrote his book in 1933 with drawings by Lansing Holden. Buckley died in Rigby, Idaho, on 13 June 1958.

James Knowles Jr was born in Cincinnati on 27 December 1897. Completing his education at Harvard he was accepted into Aviation in April 1917, and assigned to the 95th at the end of June 1918. His five victories and two probables won him the DSC and Oak Leaf, and the Croix de Guerre, plus the Aero Club of America Medal. He died in St Louis, Missouri, on 21 February 1971.

As mentioned, the other new units to fly the Nieuport 28 were the 27th and 147th Aeros, from June 1918. Donald Hudson, of the 27th, came

from Kansas City, Missouri, although he was born in Topeka on 21 December 1895. He had been with the squadron since November and remained with it until the Armistice, gaining six victories and the DSC. In 1919 he became an instructor with the Bolivian Air Force and is acknowledged as being the first pilot to fly across the Andes Mountains. He died in Maryland, 11 June 1967.

John K MacArthur was another six-victory ace with the 27th, coming from Everest, Washington, and a former electrical engineer. He was the 27th's first ace, achieved on 17 July, but a severe storm put an end to his flying three days later. Three pilots came down; two, including 'Mac', were killed. He was awarded the DSC.

Captain Jerry C Vasconcells, from Lyons, Kansas, was born on 3 December 1892. In his teens he moved to Denver, Colorado. He began a law career prior to joining the USAS and with the 27th scored six victories and won the Croix de Guerre. After becoming a flight commander, he was given command of the 185th Night Pursuit

Nieuport 28s of the 95th Aero, as flown by Sumner Sewell, L C Holden and their contemporaries *(Bruce Robertson)*

During July 1918 the 94th and 95th began replacing their Nieuports with SPAD S.XIIIs. Here Bleriot-built S.XIIIs are being assembled by American mechanics. Note the second aircraft in the hangar *(Bruce Robertson)*

John K MacArthur DSC, the 27th Aero's first ace, was killed in bad weather on 20 July 1918. He had gained his sixth victory the previous day *(Franks collection)*

Another muddy day in the life of Jerry Vasconcells and Don Hudson of the 27th Aero. Both men claimed six victories *(Franks collection)*

Squadron. He died in Denver on 17 April 1950 from a heart attack.

Zenos Ramsey Miller, the son of a Presbyterian minister, was born in Pao Ting Fu, China, on 6 October 1895, but when he joined the army he was living in Elvaston, Illinois, and attending Princeton. Transferred to aviation in 1917, he was assigned to the 27th Aero on 24 November and sailed for France. 'Red' Miller saw combat during June and July, gaining five victories before he was himself brought down and taken prisoner on 20 July, the day he became an ace. After the war he entered Princeton University and later became a doctor. However, before he began practising, he was killed in an air crash on 22 July 1922 at Framingham, Massachusetts, in a Savoia-Marchetti aircraft he had purchased. (Some sources record only four confirmed victories, and one unconfirmed.)

The two most well-known pilots in the 27th were Frank Luke Jr and Joe F Wehner, both in the SPAD period. They teamed up in September 1918 as both were somewhat at odds with their CO, and Luke in particular took a massive interest in, or dislike of, kite balloons. With Wehner often flying cover for him, Luke scored an amazing 18 kills between 12 and 29 September, 14 of them balloons, while Wehner gained six victories, five being balloons. Wehner, from Boston, born 20 September 1895, was shot down and killed on 18 September, two days before his 23rd birthday. He received two DSCs.

Luke was brought down by ground fire on the 29th. Wounded and on the wrong side of the lines, in trying to attract attention with his side-arm he was shot and killed by German soldiers. He was the only World War 1 fighter pilot to receive the Medal of Honor during the war, to add to his DSC and Oak Leaf Cluster. Luke had been born in Phoenix, Arizona, on 19 May 1897, one of nine children born of

Frank Luke Jr, balloon-buster extraordinaire with the 27th Aero is seen standing in front of his SPAD in which he was killed on 29 September 1918 after gaining his 16th, 17th and 18th kills *(Bruce Robertson)*

German immigrant parents, although his grandfather had served in the Union Army during the Civil War. Graduating from Phoenix High School he had entered the USAS in September 1917. He was assigned to the 27th Pursuit on 26 July 1918. Making his first claim over a German aircraft on 16 August, he was on his own and therefore had nobody to confirm his claim. There was also some suggestion he had been over-optimistic, and became determined to show everyone what he could do. This heralded his meteoric rise to brief fame and glory which ended in a French meadow near the village of Murvaux, on the Meuse less than six weeks later.

The 147th Pursuit Squadron produced five aces. Top scorer was Wilbert Wallace White, a married man with a young family, from New York City. The son of a Presbyterian minister, 'Wilber', as his family called him, was born on 1 May 1889. A graduate of Mercerburg Academy, Pennsylvania, in 1907 he became a student of classics at the University of Wooster, Ohio, from where he graduated in 1912. He enlisted into the

Joe Wehner of the 27th Aero was Frank Luke's flying companion until his death in combat on 18 September 1918. He had scored six victories *(Franks collection)*

SPAD S.XIIIs replaced Nieuport 28s in the 95th Aero Squadron, but the kicking mule insignia was retained *(Bruce Robertson)*

Family man Wilbert W White Jr rammed a German fighter with his SPAD S.XIII to save the life of one of his flight members and paid the supreme sacrifice, 10 October 1918. He had scored eight combat victories *(Bruce Robertson)*

Ken Porter DSC, ace of the 147th Aero, is seen standing by a Nieuport 28 (N6256) *(via Jon Guttman)*

USAS in July 1917, trained in Canada and was assigned to the 147th in February 1918. His eight victories between July and October 1918 were over four Fokkers, two Albatros Scouts, one two-seater and a balloon. These brought him the DSC and the Croix de Guerre and palm. His tour ended on 10 October 1918 but he flew two final patrols on this day, gaining his 7th victory, sharing the destruction of a Hannover CL two-seater shortly after noon, before taking off on his final mission three hours later, despite having a letter from his group commander that he could leave for home. The mission was a balloon strafe but they ran into Fokker biplanes and in the fight, his guns jammed. Seeing then a new pilot being hard pressed by a Fokker, he deliberately rammed the German fighter in order to save the novice, and fell to his death near the Meuse River. The German pilot, from *Jasta 10*, saved his life by a parachute descent, an apparatus denied to Allied airmen in the Great War. White's bravery was acknowledged by a recommendation for the Medal of Honor, but this was down-graded to a mere Oak Leaf Cluster to his DSC. In the manner of things, White was credited with the Fokker as his 8th kill, the German pilot, a SPAD for his 5th!

Four pilots achieved five victories, Ralph O'Neill, Ken Porter, James Healy and Francis Simonds. Ralph Ambrose O'Neill was of Irish descent, born in San Francisco on 7 December 1898, although he was living in Nogales, Arizona, when war came. In August 1917 he joined the USAS and after training went to the 147th in March 1918. His five victories were all shared with other pilots, but they brought him three DSCs, the Croix de Guerre and Bronze Star. After the war he went into civil aviation and died on 23 December 1980, in Redwood City, California.

Kenneth Lee Porter, born 6 December 1896, came from Dowagiac, Michigan. An engineering graduate from Michigan University,

An overturned Nieuport 28 of the 94th Aero is viewed with respectful curiosity *(Phil Jarrett)*

he joined the air service in August 1917, and was eventually assigned to the 147th in February 1918. By October he was a flight commander and had achieved his five victories over three two-seaters and two fighters – four being shared. He received the DSC and Croix de Guerre with palm. He worked with the Burroughs Business Machine Co after the war, and later the Pesco Pump Co in New York. During World War 2 he worked with Boeings on various projects before returning to engineering in 1945. He died in Jackson Heights, New York, on 3 February 1988, and is buried in Arlington Military Cemetery, Virginia.

James A Healy came from Jersey City, New Jersey, although he was born in Kansas on 26 March 1895. He too won the DSC and the Croix de Guerre and was credited with five victories, four Fokkers and a Halberstadt two-seater. He later rose to Colonel in the USAAF and died on 8 May 1893.

Francis M Simonds Jr also shared in five claims with the 147th – three fighters and two two-seaters – having been posted to this unit on 23 February 1918, staying with it until the Armistice. He received the Croix de Guerre.

THE 2ND PURSUIT GROUP

The squadrons which made up this group were the 13th, 49th, 22nd and 139th Pursuits. Its commander was Major Davenport Johnson. The 13th arrived in France in June 1918, and as mentioned earlier, its CO, Charles Biddle, gained five of his seven World War 1 victories with it. Other than him, four pilots became aces, three with six kills, one with five.

Murray Keith Guthrie, from Mobile, Alabama, was born on 29 May 1896 in Minnesota. His six victories – all over Fokker biplanes – brought him the DSC with two Oak Leaf Clusters. He lived until 1985, dying in Texas.

Frank Kerr Hays was born in Louisville, Kentucky, on 3 November 1896. Living in Chicago when he joined the USAS, he was assigned to the 13th on 29 August 1918. His first three claims were made in one action on 13 September, a fourth two days later – all shared. Two Fokkers on

W H 'Hank' Stovall was the son of an American Civil War colonel. He shot down two Albatros and four Fokker fighters to achieve acedom in the 13th Aero *(Franks collection via Stovall family)*

4 November made him an ace. That first action won for him the DSC, for he had continued in action despite jammed guns, and having cleared them went on to save his flight commander who was under serious attack. Hays died in Carmel, California, on 9 March 1988.

William H Stovall came from Stovall, Mississippi, born in 1895, on the family cotton plantation, the son of a civil war colonel. Graduating from Lawrenceville School, New Jersey, in 1913 he moved to Yale in 1916. Assigned to the 13th Aero in July 1918, 'Hank' Stovall shot down two Albatros and four Fokker fighters between 1 August and 23 October and received the DSC. After the war he returned to the family plantation and in World War 2 again served his country as a Major in the USAAC, becoming director of personnel with the US 8th Air Force in England. He later became Chief of Staff under his old wartime comrade in the 13th, General Carl Spaatz. For this war he received the Legion of Merit, Bronze Star, Légion d'Honneur and the Croix de Guerre, and became an Officer of the Order of the British Empire by the British. After a successful life in the plantation business, he died in his sleep at his home on 11 May 1970.

John J Seerley, from Chicago, Illinois, arrived at the 13th Pursuit on 5 July 1918. That summer he shared in five victories which afforded him the title of ace.

In the 22nd Squadron there were five aces by the war's end. It was commanded by Captain Ray C Bridgeman who had flown with the French. Top scorer was Jacques Michael Swaab, from Philadelphia, born 21 April 1894. With the 22nd he flew in all the major actions on the

Jacques Swaab's snowbound SPAD S.XIII, 22nd Aero Squadron, one of the 893 S.XIIIs America purchased from the French. The 22nd Aero was declared operational on 22 August 1918 and boasted five aces by the war's end *(US National Archives)*

French/American front – Toul, St Mihiel and Argonne offensives, and although he didn't arrive on the Squadron till 27 August 1918, by the end of October he had scored ten victories, with possibly another seven unconfirmed. He won the DSC and, on the first war patrol over the lines, downed three German aircraft. After the war he was in Hollywood and became technical adviser to the film *Dawn Patrol*, starring Errol Flynn and David Niven. He died in Los Angeles on 7 July 1963 and is another old warrior buried in Arlington Military Cemetery.

Top scorer with the 22nd Aero was Jacques M Swaab from Philadelphia. On his first patrol over the lines he downed three German aircraft. By the end of October 1918 he had shot down ten German aircraft with another seven unconfirmed *(Bruce Robertson)*

Eight victories were claimed by Clinton S Jones Jr, from San Francisco, California, born on New Year's Day 1892. He arrived at the 22nd Squadron on 27 August 1918 and his first victory was a third share in a Fokker biplane on 4 September. Two more Fokkers fell to his guns on 28 September and during October he downed four two-seaters, two shared, two on his own. These victories brought him the DSC and Oak Leaf. He survived the war and died in Sacramento, on 23 June 1965.

James D Beane was mentioned earlier, due to his early flying with the Lafayette Flying Corps. His six kills brought him acedom with the 22nd Aero. Likewise, Remington Vernam was covered earlier, but scored victories two through to six with the 22nd Aero.

Captain A R Brooks also downed six – all with the 22nd. Arthur 'Ray' Brooks, born 1 November 1895, came from Framingham, Massachusetts, and attended MIT (Massachusetts Institute of Technology), from where he graduated in 1917. Straight away he enlisted into the air service, completing his training with the British in Canada. His first squadron was the 139th where he gained one victory on 29 July 1918 prior to moving to the 22nd as a flight commander on 16 August. He shot down a two-seater

This SPAD S.XIII of the 22nd Aero Squadron was possibly flown by James D Beane, who flew both with the Lafayette Flying Corps and with the 22nd Aero *(Bruce Robertson)*

Ray Brooks gained his six victories with the 139th and 22nd Aero Squadrons in 1918. He served with the USAAC in World War 2 and died in 1991 at the age of 95 *(E F Cheesman)*

Karl Schoen of the 139th Aero by his SPAD S.XIII (No 13). Note the lucky swastika emblem between the 1 and the 3, and the name 'René' *(Franks collection)*

on 2 September, then shared three Fokkers and another two-seater by the war's end (with four more unconfirmed), which brought him the DSC (although he too had been recommended for the Medal of Honor). He took command of the 22nd after the Armistice and was made captain. Back in the US he remained with the Air Service until late 1922. He served in the USAAC in World War 2 and later became Publications Manager to the Bell Telephone Company in New Jersey. He died in Summit, NJ, on 17 July 1991 and as far as is known he was the last surviving USAS ace of World War 1. He also received the Silver Star and the Aero Club of America's Medal of Merit.

The 139th Squadron was commanded by Major Lawrence C Angstrom. Like the 27th and 147th Squadrons, its pilots had all been trained in Canada and then Texas. Angstrom himself had come via the British RFC, having been wounded with No 25 Squadron in June 1916 as a 2nd Lieutenant. He joined the 2nd Pursuit Group in late June 1918. The squadron produced six aces, the highest scorers being Wendel A Robertson and Karl J Schoen, each with seven kills.

Wendel Robertson came from Fort Smith, Arkansas, and it is unfortunate that little is known about him. He shot down four Pfalz Scouts and three Fokker biplanes between 10 September and 30 October, all shared with other pilots. He was probably decorated but with what is unknown. One thing that is known is that he was in the same air fight on 12 September in which flight commander David Putnam was killed, Putnam having scored four victories with the 139th to add to his nine scored with the French.

Karl Schoen Jr came from Indianapolis, Indiana, born 20 October 1896. He joined the 139th on 13 February 1918 and worked-up with the unit. During September and October he helped shoot down seven German aircraft – five fighters and two two-seaters – before being killed in action south of Damvillers on 29 October, in a fight in which he assisted in downing two Fokkers. His DSC was awarded posthumously.

Robert Opie Lindsay, from Madison, North Carolina, was born on Christmas Day, 1894. Bob Lindsay joined the 139th on 20 August 1918 and his six victories were five assists and one lone kill. He received the DSC and survived the war. Later he saw service with the USAF, retiring with the rank of colonel. He died on 1 August 1952.

Three pilots gained five victories: H H George, E M Haight and J S Owens. Harold Huston George came from Niagara Falls, New York State, although he was born 19 July 1893 in Lockport, NY. He did not arrive in the 139th until 16 September 1918 but shared in five victories during October and November, and received the DSC. During World War 2 he gained high rank with the USAAC but died from injuries received in a aeroplane crash at Darwin, Australia, on 30 April 1942.

Edward M Haight was born 30 May 1896 and came from Astoria, New York. He had served with the 49th for three days before arriving at the 139th Pursuit on 17 August 1918. His five victories were all over fighters, four being shared kills, and he later became a colonel in the USAF. Haight died on 5 December 1975.

John Sidney Owens hailed from Baltimore, Maryland. He was assigned to the 139th on 5 February 1918 while they were still working up for combat. His five victories were all shared with other pilots. During World War 2 he became a lieutenant-colonel in the USAAC and died at Coral Gables, Florida, on 14 January 1965.

THE 3RD PURSUIT GROUP

The Squadron which made up the 3rd Group – commanded by Bill Thaw – were the 93rd, 213th and the 28th Pursuits; later joined by the 103rd. Major John Huffer's 93rd Squadron began operations on 11 August 1918 and its three months of combat flying produced three aces. Huffer himself had been in the Lafayette Flying Corps and gained three (or four) official and four (or three) unconfirmed.

Top scorer was Chester E Wright from Readville, Massachusetts, born 1 September 1897. having completed three years at Harvard, Wright joined the USAS in March 1917, and continued training at MIT. Later in the year he became adjutant of the 19th Aero in New York, then sailed for Europe in November. Completing his training he first became a ferry pilot before going to the 93rd on 29 July. The following month, as operations began, he became a flight commander. He won the two DSCs for his nine confirmed victories, which included one balloon, and returned home in March 1919.

Leslie J Rummell, from Newark, NJ, was born 21 February 1895. Known as 'Rummy' he joined the 93rd Squadron on 7 August 1918. His seven victories – six Fokkers and one two-seater – brought him the DSC post-war but he died on 2 February 1919 in the influenza epidemic that swept the world.

Charles Rudolph D'Olive was born in Suggsville, Alabama, on 10 July 1896 and later lived in Cedar Falls, Iowa. From here he enlisted into the air service in Memphis in April 1917, went to France to complete his training and was then assigned to the 93rd Aero on 23 August 1918. He shot down

Bob Lindsay achieved six victories with the 139th Aero
(Franks collection)

Top scorer of the 93rd Aero was Chester E Wright, who claimed nine victories during the autumn of 1918
(E F Cheesman)

Chester Wright , in front of his SPAD
S.XIII, which sports the 93rd's Indian
head insignia
(Franks collection)

Leslie J Rummell brought down
seven hostile aircraft whilst serving
with the 93rd Aero in late 1918,
although he survived the war only
by a few weeks, dying of influenza
in February 1919 (Franks collection)

five Fokker biplanes (including the
unit's first victory on 12 September)
before being transferred to the 141st
Squadron on 28 October as a flight
commander, but this unit hardly got
into action before the war ended. He
received the DSC and left the service
in 1919 and went into business. He
died from cancer on 20 July 1974.
For some reason it took some years
to confirm him as an ace despite his
DSC citation mentioning three victories on 13 September 1918 which,
added to his two other kills, made
him an ace. Therefore, he was the
last World War 1 fighter ace to be
officially acknowledged – in 1963 –
45 years after becoming one!

The 213th Squadron, com-
manded by 1/Lt John Hamilton,
previously with the 95th, began
operations on 14 August 1918. Its
one ace was Charles Gossage Grey, a
former member of the Lafayette
Flying Corps (see Chapter 3). He
arrived at the 213th on 1 August
1918. His five victories – three
Fokkers, one two-seater and a
balloon – brought him the DSC and
made him a flight commander,
with promotion to Captain on
6 November.

The 28th Pursuit Squadron was commanded by Captain Charles
Maury Jones, a former flight commander with the 13th Aero. This unit
began operations on 2 September 1918 and produced one ace.

Charles D'Olive (left) with Capt
Hobart Baker of the 141st Aero. The
first to score a victory for the 93rd
Aero, D'Olive was the last World
War 1 fighter ace to be officially
acknowleged – 45 years later. Baker
was killed in a crash on 21
December 1918 (Franks collection)

Martinus Stenseth was born in Heiberg on 11 June 1890 and lived in Twin Valley, Minnesota. A corporal in the Minnesota National Guard, he later joined the air service. He was assigned to the 28th on 27 August 1918 and between 26 September and 6 November, downed eight German aircraft and received the DSC. He commanded the squadron briefly after the war then saw service in the Baltic with the American Relief Association before returning home. Back in the States he commanded the 147th Squadron in Texas. Remaining in the air force he rose to Brigadier General after World War 2, receiving the Silver Star, and commanding Nellis Air Force Base, Nevada, both during and after the war. He died in nearby Las Vegas on 25 June 1979.

Another ace to fly with the 28th was flight commander Tom Cassady, who was covered earlier with the French *Escadrille* SPA 163. He shot down four aircraft with the 28th Pursuit making his World War 1 total victories nine.

— The Lafayette Squadron in the USAS —

Once N 124 came under the control of the Americans and changed its identity to the 103rd Pursuit Squadron USAS it lost much of its old character. It had already started to equip with SPADs way back in 1917 and in 1918 it had the SPAD XIII. It also remained with the French *Groupe de Chasse 21* until April. Its first CO was Bill Thaw, who added three kills to his *Lafayette* score to become an ace. On 1 July 1918 the 103rd Squadron came under USAS control to become part of the 3rd Pursuit Group.

Charles Biddle gained his seventh and final victory with the 103rd and, of course, Lieutenants Larner and Ponder, as previously mentioned, added to their earlier scores to become aces while flying combat with the 103rd.

Paul Frank Baer, from Fort Wayne, Indiana, was born in January 1895, had joined the Lafayette Flying Corps in 1917 and had been with the French SPA 80 from August to January 1918, then went to N 124. He did not claim any victories until the unit had become the 103rd Aero but then, between 11 March and 22 May, he claimed nine confirmed and seven probable victories, to win the DSC with Oak Leaf Cluster, and the Croix

de Guerre. His victory of 11 March over an Albatros Scout was the first success by a USAS pilot. As he gained his 9th victory on 22 May he was himself shot down during a fight with *Jasta 18* over Armentières, and taken into captivity. In April 1919 the French made him a Chevalier of the Légion d'Honneur. He continued to fly after the war and was killed in an air crash in Hong Kong harbour on 9 December 1930.

As the summer progressed, the 103rd produced three more aces of its own. Frank O'Driscoll Hunter came from Savannah, Georgia,

107 (94) Paul Baer flew with the 103rd Aero after serving with the French, scoring the USAS's first victory on 22 May 1918. He achieved nine victories in all before being taken prisoner after combat with *Jasta 18* over Armentières on 22 May 1918 (E F Cheesman)

born December 1894. Graduating from Hotchkiss School in 1913 he enlisted into the US Aviation Section in 1917, trained in the US and in France and was assigned to the 94th Aero in May 1918. Within a week he was reassigned to the 103rd with whom he later became a flight commander. 'Monk', as he was known, gained nine victories – seven Fokker biplanes and two two-seaters – and won the DSC and four Oak Leaves as well as the Légion d'Honneur. He remained in the US Air Force, did some mail service flying, becoming a Major in 1936

Frank O'D Hunter gained all nine of his victories with the 103rd Aero. He remained in the US Air Force, rising to the rank of Major General in World War 2 *(Franks collection)*

and a Colonel just as America entered World War 2. He was also an air attaché in London at one time. During World War 2 he rose to Major-General and commanded the US 8th Air Force's Fighter Command in England. He finally retired from the service in 1946, returning to his native Savannah, where he died in June 1982.

Edgar Tobin, born 1895, came from San Antonio, Texas. He gained six victories with the 103rd between 11 July and 28 September 1918, plus at least one probable. Cited in General Orders, he also received the DSC. He was killed in a flying accident in a Grumman Mallard on 10 January 1954, on Lake Wallace, near Shreveport, Louisiana, aged 58.

From Rochester, Minnesota, George W Furlow enlisted into the USAS in 1917 and was assigned to the 103rd on 25 July 1918. Between then and the Armistice he accounted for five German aircraft and won the DSC and Oak Leaf Cluster.

A Camel of the 148th Aero Squadron *c* 1918, down in no-man's-land *(Phil Jarrett)*

OTHER AMERICAN ACES

The United States Air Service designated several other airmen as aces in World War 1, from pilots and gunners of two-seater units, either bombing squadrons or those engaged in reconnaissance.

William Terry Badham, from Birmingham, Alabama, was born 27 September 1895. He served as an observer/gunner with the French before being reassigned to the American 91st Observation Squadron on 28 May 1918 flying Salmson 2A 2 two-seaters. With the 91st he was credited with five victories in company with his pilots. The first victory, over a Pfalz Scout, was shared with Lieutenant George C Kenny, who in World War 2 would command the US 5th Air Force in the Pacific. Badham's next four kills were with Captain Everett R Cook, CO of the 91st. Badham received the DSC and after the war worked in his father's coal mining business. He died in Mentone, Alabama, on 6 June 1991.

Everett Richard Cook himself had been born in Indianapolis, Indiana, on 13 December 1894, although he later lived in Memphis, Tennessee. Joining the Air Service in May 1917 he took command of the 91st Aero in September 1918. Five accredited victories won him the DSC, Légion d'Honneur and the Croix de Guerre with palm. Not long after the war Cook was on the staff of General Billy Mitchell, and upon leaving the service became a member of the Cotton Exchange in Memphis, and later in 1931, its President. In World War 2 he received the Silver Star and Legion of Merit for his service with the US 8th Air Force in both England and the Middle East, as a brigadier-general. After that war he was on the Board of Eastern Airlines with Eddie Rickenbacker. He died on 21 January 1974 in Memphis.

Lt E R Cook, CO 91st Aero, used this personally marked SPAD S.XIII (15564); his unit flew Salmson 2A 2 machines *(US National Archives via Phil Jarrett)*

Arthur E Easterbrook was credited with five victories as an observer flying Salmson 2A 2s with the 1st Aero Squadron in late 1918, after serving with the RAF
(Franks collection)

Pilot William P Erwin was credited with his observers with eight victories flying Salmson 2A 2s with the 1st Aero Squadron in late 1918
(Franks collection)

Arthur E Easterbrook came from Fort Flager, Washington, although he was born in Amsterdam, New York, on 4 November 1893. His first actions were whilst flying with the RAF in No 9 Squadron, as an observer in R.E.8 two-seaters. Reassigned to the USAS he joined the 1st Observation Squadron on 20 August 1918 and the following month, during the St Mihiel battle, he was awarded the DSC for bravery during a recce mission behind the German front lines. Flying Salmsons with Lt William P Erwin, Easterbrook claimed four combat victories in October and with another pilot downed number five on 4 November. He died on 24 July 1952 at Long Beach, California, following a bad fall the previous year.

William P Erwin, Easterbrook's pilot, added another four victories whilst flying with other observers, making a total of eight. He was born in Amarillo, Texas, but was living in Chicago when war came. He won the

DSC for his work with the 1st Aero and the Croix de Guerre. Erwin disappeared during the Dole Air Races from Oakland, California, to Hawaii on 18 October 1927, it being assumed he had come down somewhere over the Pacific Ocean.

James A Keating was born on 4 December 1897, in Chicago, Illinois. With the USAS he became part of the Toronto Group of trainees and was sent to No 49 Squadron RAF for experience and won the British DFC on 9 August 1918. With his observer on that day, he was credited with downing four Fokker biplanes, and having claimed a Pfalz D.III the previous day, this bag made them both aces, Keating also receiving a DSC from his own country. He died on 2 October 1976.

Major Victor Herbert Strahm, from Evanston, Illinois, was born on 26 October 1895 in Nashville, Tennessee. He was a pilot with the 91st Observation Squadron from 22 February 1918 until the Armistice, and with his observers was credited with five air victories between 4 September and 4 November. His DSC was awarded for a particularly dangerous mission flown on 13 September, 25 kilometres behind the German lines and at less than 300 feet, despite ground fire and hostile aircraft. Later in the USAAC he rose to the rank of brigadier-general and was also a test pilot. He died at Shreveport, Louisiana, on 11 May 1957.

James A Keating flew with No 49 Squadron RAF and with his observers was credited with five victories in August 1918, including four Fokker biplanes in one day *(Franks collection)*

112 (101) Victor H Strahm was credited with five victories with his observers, flying as a pilot with the 91st Observation Squadron in late 1918. The insignia of the knight on a charger was that of the 91st Aero. Strahm later became a test pilot *(Franks collection)*

United States Air Service Aces by Squadron

Squadron	Name	Score	Notes
13th Pursuit	Lt M K Guthrie	6	
	Lt F K Hays	6	
	Lt W H Stovall	6	
	Maj C J Biddle	5(7)	French Air Service
	Lt J J Seerley	5	
17th Pursuit	Lt H Burdick	8	
	Lt H C Knotts	6	PoW 14 Oct 1918
	Lt G A Vaughn Jr	6(13)	84 Sqn RAF
	Lt L A Hamilton	5(10)	3 Sqn RAF, KIA 24 Aug 18
	Lt R M Todd	5	PoW 26 Aug 1918
	Lt W D Tipton	3(5)	PoW 26 Aug 1918
22nd Pursuit	Capt J M Swaab	10	
	Lt C S Jones Jr	8	
	Lt J D Beane	6	
	Capt A R Brooks	6	
	Lt R DeB Vernam	5(6)	PoW 30 Oct 1918 - DoW
27th Pursuit	Lt F Luke Jr	18	KIA 29 Sept 1918
	Lt D Hudson	6	
	Lt J K MacArthur	6	Killed 20 July 1918
	Capt J C Vasconcells	6	
	Lt J Wehner	6	KIA 18 Sept 1918
28th Pursuit	Lt M Stenseth	7	
	Capt T G Cassady	4(9)	French Air Service
93rd Pursuit	Lt C E Wright	9	
	Lt L J Rummell	7	Died 2 Feb 1919
94th Pursuit	Capt E V Rickenbacker	26	
	Capt H Coolidge	8	KIA 27 Oct 1918
	Capt R M Chambers	7	
	Lt H W Cook	7	
	Lt D Campbell	6	WIA 5 Jun 1918
	Capt D McPeterson	5(6)	French Air Service
	Lt J A Meissner	4(8)	147th Aero
95th Pursuit	Lt L C Holden Jr	7	
	Lt S Sewell	7	
	Lt E P Curtis	6	
	Lt H R Buckley	5	
	Lt J Knowles Jr	5	

103rd Pursuit	Lt P F Baer	9	PoW 22 May 1918
	Lt F O'D Hunter	8	
	Lt E G Tobin	6	
	Lt G W Furlow	5	
	Lt G de F Larner	5(7)	French Air Service
	Lt W T Ponder	3(6)	French Air Service
	Maj W Thaw	3(5)	Lafayette Escadrille
	Maj C Biddle	1(7)	French Air Service
139th Pursuit	Lt W A Robertson	7	
	Lt K Schoen Jr	7	KIA 29 Oct 1918
	Lt R O Lindsay	6	
	Lt H H George	5	
	Lt E M Haight	5	
	Lt J S Owens	5	
	Capt D E Putnam	4(13)	French Air Service
147th Pursuit	Lt W W White Jr	8	KIA 10 Oct 1918
	Lt R O'Neill	5	
	Lt K L Porter	5	
	Lt J A Healy	5	
	Lt F M Simonds Jr	5	
	Capt J A Meissner	4(8)	94th Aero
148th Pursuit	Capt E W Springs	12(16)	85 Sqn RAF
	Capt F E Kindley	11(12)	65 Sqn RAF
	Lt H R Clay Jr	8	Died 17 Feb 1919
	Lt J O Creech	8	
	Capt C L Bissell	5	
	Lt A O Ralston	3(5)	85 Sqn RAF
	Lt L K Callahan	2(5)	85 Sqn RAF
213rd Pursuit	Capt C G Grey	5	

Figure in brackets indicates total WWI victories

American Aces with the French Air Service only

Escadrille Spa.3	Lt F L Baylies	12
Escadrille Spa.157/163	Adj J A Connelly Jr	7
Escadrille N.124	Maj G R Lufbery	16
Escadrille N.124/Spa.3	Lt E C Parsons	8

American Aces with British Squadrons

24 Squadron RAF	Lt H L Bair	6	
20 Squadron RFC/RAF	Capt W Beaver	19	
40 Squadron RAF	Lt L Bennett Jr	12	KIA 24 Aug 1918
64 Squadron RAF	Lt C A Bissonette	6	
66 Squadron RAF	Lt H K Boyson	5	
29 Squadron RAF	Lt S M Brown	5	
210 Squadron RAF	Lt A Buchanan	7	
32 Squadron RAF	Capt A A Callender	8	KIA 30 Oct 1918
45 Squadron RAF	Lt C G Catto	6	
11 Squadron RAF	Lt E S Coler	16	
73 Squadron RAF	Lt N Cooper	6	
32 Squadron RAF	Capt J O Donaldson	7	PoW 1 Sep 1918
79 Squadron RAF	Capt F W Gillet	20	
60 Squadron RAF	Lt J S Griffith	7	
32 Squadron RAF	Capt F L Hale	7	
29 Squadron RFC	Lt D'A F Hilton	8	
208 Squadron RAF	Lt M C Howell	5	
20 Squadron RAF	Lt A T Iaccaci	17	WIA Sept 1918
20 Squadron RAF	Lt P T Iaccaci	17	
213 Squadron RAF	Lt D S Ingalls	6	
1 Squadron RAF	Lt D Knight	10	
1 Squadron RAF	Capt H A Kullberg	19	
24 Squadron RAF	Capt W C Lambert	18	
40 Squadron RAF	Maj R G Landis	12	
84 Squadron RAF	Lt J F Larsen	9	
209 Squadron RAF	Capt O C LeBoutillier	10	
23/11/43/25 Sqns RFC/RAF	Capt F Libby	14	
79 Squadron RAF	Capt F I Lord	12	
74 Squadron RAF	Lt F E Luff	5	
73 Squadron RAF	Capt E J Lussier	11	
1 Squadron RAF	Lt F P Magoun	5	WIA 10 Apr 1918
23 Squadron RAF	Capt J W Pearson	11	
210 Squadron RAF	Lt C F Pineau	6	PoW 8 Oct 1918
32 Squadron RAF	Lt B Rogers	6	
92 Squadron RAF	Capt O J Rose	16	
74 Squadron RAF	Lt H G Shoemaker	5	Killed 6 Oct 1918
139 Squadron RAF	Lt W K Simon	8	
79 Squadron RAF	Lt E Taylor	5	KIA 24 Aug 1918
210 Squadron RAF	Lt K R Unger	14	
23 Squadron RFC	Capt C W Warman	12	WIA 20 Aug 1917
23 Squadron RAF	Lt H A White	6	

American Two-seater pilot/observer Aces

91st Aero	Lt W T Badham	5
91st Aero	Capt E R Cook	5
1st Aero	Lt A E Easterbrook	5
1st Aero	Lt W P Erwin	8
9 Squadron RAF	Lt J A Keating	5
91st Aero	Maj V H Strahm	5

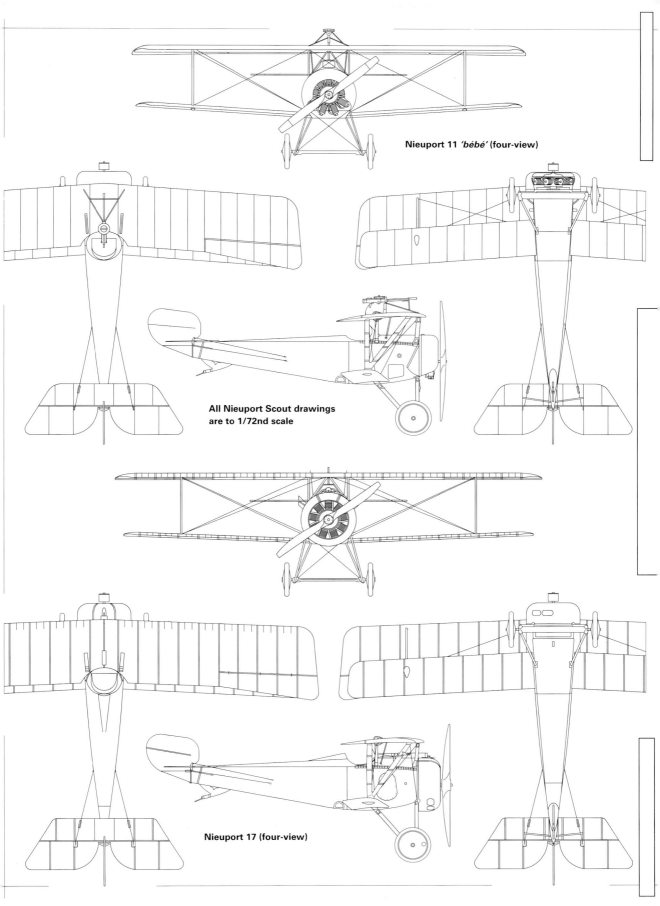

Nieuport 11 *'bébé'* (four-view)

All Nieuport Scout drawings
are to 1/72nd scale

Nieuport 17 (four-view)

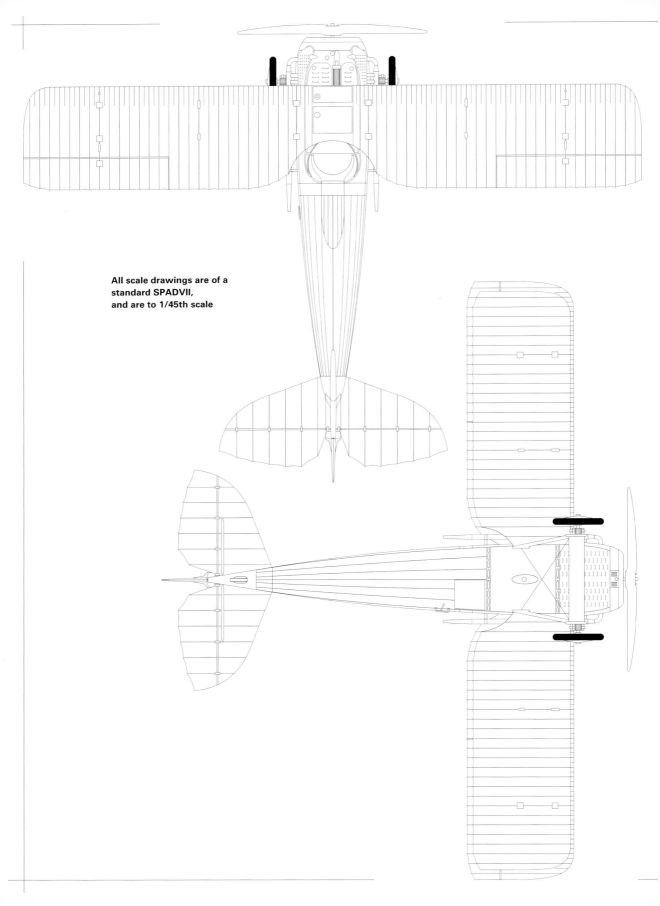

All scale drawings are of a
standard SPADVII,
and are to 1/45th scale

COLOUR PLATES

1

Nieuport 11 N1256 flown by Sgt G R Lufbery, *Lafayette Escadrille* N124, 1916

Believed to have been the first aircraft used by Raoul Lufbery in the *Escadrille*, N1256 bore the sprayed-on upper surface camouflage used on many of the early French Nieuport Scouts in two-tone dark brown and greyish-green in large patterns. Undersurfaces remained in clear dope or sometimes pale blue. The engine cowling remained unpainted aluminium. Lufbery's personal emblem was the stylised RL monogram.

2

Nieuport 17 flown by Lt E C Parsons, *Lafayette Escadrille* N124, 1916

Ed Parsons flew with the *Lafayette Escadrille* and SPA 3. The aircraft is in standard aluminium doped finish with Parsons' personal initials ECP in red on the fuselage. Kenneth Marr crashed this machine later, overshooting on landing and ending upside down on a railway embankment by the airfield.

3

SPAD VII S1456 flown by Lt W Thaw, *Lafayette Escadrille* SPA 124, April 1917

After converting from Nieuports to SPADs, Bill Thaw continued to use his personal initial T on the fuselage of his machines. He gained his first two victories with the *Escadrille* before transferring to the USAS, taking command of the squadron as it became the 103rd Aero. Thaw was flying S1456 when he downed an Albatros two-seater over Neuville on 26 April 1917 for his second victory.

4

SPAD VII S1777 flown by Sous-Lt G Raoul Lufbery, *Lafayette Escadrille* SPA124, December 1917

Pilots used any number of machines and Raoul Lufbery did so too. While it appears he often changed personal markings, in reality pilots often shared aircraft depending on the availability. This SPAD VII, previously used by Didier Masson, carried the good luck symbol of a red swastika on the fuselage. The fabric was clear doped and varnished which gave a sandy/yellow appearance. The metal cowling areas were painted a glossy yellow to match. Lufbery claimed victories 13, 14 and 16 in this machine.

5

SPAD VII flown by Major C J Biddle, SPA 73, late 1917

The camouflage was standard fawn with a red letter '8' towards the end of the fuselage. SPA 73's insignia was a *cigogne* (stork) over a diagonal blue and white fuselage band, part of the Storks Group – GC12. Biddle moved on to the 103rd Aero and later became commander of the 13th Aero, ending the war with seven confirmed victories.

6

SPAD VII flown by 1st Lt Thomas G Cassady, SPA 163, early 1918

Cassady transferred from the Lafayette Flying Corps to the US Air Service in February 1918 where he was assigned to 103rd Aero then to SPA 163 in the following May. Between May and September he downed five enemy planes before joining the 28th Aero as flight leader, where he added four more victories to his score.

7

SPAD XIII flown by Caporal Gorman deFreest Larner, SPA 86, early 1918

The aircraft has standard French camouflage with the unit's insignia of a winged star on the fuselage; '13' was Larner's lucky number. He used the same number when he transferred to the 103rd Aero Squadron, ending the war as a lieutenant with seven confirmed victories.

8

SPAD XIII S15557 flown by Lt William T Ponder, 103rd Aero Squadron, late 1918

The Kellner-built aircraft has standard camouflage overall together with the 103rd's Indian head insignia and Ponder's individual number '24' on the fuselage. Ponder flew with SPA 67 and SPA 163 before moving to the 103rd Aero Squadron in September 1918.

9

SE5a B189 flown by 1st Lt R G Landis, No 40 Squadron RAF, May 1918

Reed Landis claimed his first victory on 8 May 1918 in this aircraft: a Pfalz DIII. The aircraft was marked with an 'S' on the tail fin above the serial number. The 'S' was repeated on the top port wing. B189 was later flown by two other British aces, W L Harrison and J H Tudhope, who both scored kills with it.

10

SE5a C1835 flown by Lt H A Kullberg, No 1 Squadron RAF, summer 1918

Harold Kullberg claimed seven of his 19 combat victories in this aircraft. Painted in standard RAF camouflage, the aircraft carried the Squadron marking of a small white circle aft of the fuselage roundel and the individual letter 'T'. The serial number is stencilled in white on the rudder.

11

SE5a C1106 flown by Lt Duerson Knight, No 1 Squadron RAF, summer 1918

'Dewey' Knight claimed three of his ten victories in this machine in early June 1918, one of which was a Fokker Triplane of *Jasta* 14 which he helped to bring down inside Allied lines on 9 June. It carries the white circle of No 1 Squadron and the individual letter 'Y'.

12

SE5a D6991 flown by Lt B Rogers, No 32 Squadron RAF, summer 1918

Bogart Rogers scored two victories in this machine on 6 September, and his 6th and last on 1 November. The two small inverted white bars are the Squadron's identification marking. The White 'A' forward of the cockpit was the Flight marking (A, B or C Flight). In 1918 these letters were repeated on the top starboard wing midway between the centre section and the roundel, while each individual aircraft was identified by a number in a similar position on the port wing.

13

SE5 D6851 flown by Lt E W Springs, No 85 Squadron RAF, June 1918

Elliot White Springs gained four of his 16 victories with this unit, three of them in this aircraft. Oddly, whilst 85's machines usually repeated the individual letter, in this case an 'X', on the top starboard wing, this machine when photographed on 21 June shows the letter 'T' on the top wing. The white hexagon is the Squadron marking. Springs' other 12 victories were as a flight commander with the 148th Aero Squadron.

14

Sopwith Dolphin C3824 flown by Lt J W Pearson, No 23 Squadron RAF, 1918

J W Pearson gained the first three of his eleven victories in this machine. The individual letter 'U' on the fuselage was repeated on the top fuselage decking and on the top port wing. The Squadron marking of a white circle on the fuselage was also repeated on the top starboard wing.

15

Sopwith Dolphin C3887 flown by Lt F W Gillet, No 79 Squadron RAF, August 1918

Fred Gillet gained his first three victories flying this aircraft during August 1918. The individual letter 'F' is, unusually, painted on the fuselage between the roundel and the Squadron's white square marking. Gillet was the highest scoring ace in No 79 Squadron with a total of 20 victories – the last three on 10 November 1918 the day before the Armistice.

16

Sopwith Dolphin D3727 flown by Lt E Taylor, No 79 Squadron RAF, 1918

Edgar Taylor scored all of his five victories in this machine during the month of August and was killed in it on the 24th of the month. The individual letter 'J' was repeated on the top starboard wing just inboard of the roundel.

17

Sopwith Camel F6034 flown by Lt G A Vaughn, 17th Aero Squadron, 1918

The aircraft has standard RAF camouflage with the white dumbell marking of the 17th, and the individual letter 'N' forward of the fuselage. The machine has white wheel covers (indicating B Flight) and white cowling (George Vaughan's own flight commander marking). Vaughan shot down two Fokker DVIIs in this machine on 22 September, but was then shot down by Ltn Friedrich Noltenius of *Jasta* 17. This was a rebuilt machine, formerly C6708 of No 46 Squadron in which Lt E R Watt claimed three victories.

18

Sopwith Camel D8250 flown by Capt E W Springs, 148th Aero Squadron, 1918

The aircraft has standard RAF camouflage with the 148th white triangle marking on the fuselage and Elliot White Springs' individual aircraft letter 'O' forward of the fuselage roundel. Springs claimed at least eight of his twelve victories during August and September 1918 in this machine.

19

Sopwith Camel D9438 flown by Lt E J Lussier, No 73 Squadron RAF, 1918

Emile Lussier was the most successful American Camel pilot flying with the British. The individual letter was 'D' (and may have been 'B' earlier). D9438 had standard camouflage and has the unit insignia of two thin vertical white lines after of the roundel.

20

Sopwith Camel D6519 flown by Lt Lloyd A Hamilton, No 3 Squadron RAF, spring 1918

Lloyd Hamilton accounted for five enemy aircraft between April and June 1918, gaining at least two of his victories in this machine. After transferring to 17th Aero he had brought his score up to ten by the time of his death in action on 24 August. The No 3 Squadron insignia of two vertical white bands are shown aft of the fuselage roundel.

21

Sopwith Camel E1539 flown by Capt F E Kindley, 148th Aero Squadron, 1918

Field Kindley originally flew Camels with the RAF before moving to the 148th. He scored seven of his 12 victories in this machine during September and October 1918. The aircraft is in standard RAF camouflage. The white triangle aft of the fuselage roundel is the Squadron marking of the 148th.

22

Sopwith Camel C3312 flown by Lt N Cooper, No 73 Squadron RAF, summer 1918

C3312 individual letter 'Y' was the mount of Norman Cooper, who flew with No 73 Squadron in the summer of 1918. The profile shows the Squadron marking of two thin white vertical bands aft of the fuselage roundel. Cooper gained victories five and six in this machine on 15 September.

23
Sopwith Camel F2141 flown by Lt H Burdick, 17th Aero Squadron, 1918
Howard Burdick was the highest scoring ace in the 17th with eight confirmed kills. F2141 had standard camouflage with grey engine cowling and the white individual letter 'L' between the cockpit and the roundel. The wheel covers were white, denoting B Flight. The serial number was marked on the rudder and the fuselage, although the latter was partly overpainted by the dumbell Squadron marking of the 17th. Burdick gained five of his victories in this machine.

24
Sopwith Camel E1586 flown by Lt H R Clay Jr, 148th Aero Squadron, 1918
Henry Clay had used 'S' as his individual marking on Camel D8180 to gain his first four victories. In E1586 he added four more to bring his final score to eight. The 148th's white triangle was marked aft of the fuselage roundel, with the serial number on the rudder, and again he used 'S' as his personal marking.

25
Sopwith Camel F3930 flown by Lt K R Unger, No 210 Squadron RAF, 1918
Kenneth Unger used F3930 to score seven of his 14 victories during the autumn of 1918. It carried the individual letter 'U' below the cockpit. The Squadron identification mark was a white circle aft of the fuselage roundel. This was repeated on the top starboard wing near the centre section.

26
Nieuport 28 N6164 flown by Lt D Campbell, 94th Aero Squadron, spring 1918
Douglas Campbell made history as the first American-trained ace flying with the 94th. He claimed his first victory, on 14 April 1918, in this Nieuport scout D6164. Note the red and black petal design on the engine cowling. The individual number '10' can be seen aft of the famous Hat-in-Ring insignia of the 94th. The aircraft is in standard five-colour French camouflage for this period, with buff undersides, blue headrest and whole rudder in national colours.

27
Nieuport 28 N6169 flown by Lt E V Rickenbacker, 94th Aero Squadron, early 1918
All US-flown Nieuport 28s were painted in the French five-colour camouflage. The red, white and blue fin/rudder colours (with red at the rear) were now in keeping with the American wing cockades, which were red, blue and white as opposed to the French red, white and blue. The individual number '1' is shadow-edged in red. The American 'ace of aces' also used aircraft '12' and 16'. N6169 had previously been used by Major John Huffer, the 94th's first CO.

28
Nieuport 28 N6144 flown by Lt James Meissner, 94th

Aero Squadron, 1918
Jimmy Meissner scored his first four victories in this machine. It was originally marked 'dark 14' before becoming 'white 8'. It carried a Liberty Loan poster stuck to the lower right wing's upper surface just out from the wing-root. Meissner's machine twice shed its top wing fabric, on 2 and 30 May.

29
Nieuport 28 N6256 flown by Lt K L Porter, 147th Aero Squadron, 1918
The individual number was a black '15' edged in white, repeated in black on the starboard upper wing. On the opposite wing was a large 'C' indicating the Flight, a practice which was not carried over to the unit's SPADS later. Cowling and wheel covers were thought to be blue.

30
SPAD XIII S18869 flown by Capt J M Swaab, 22nd Aero Squadron, 1918
Jacques Swaab used this SPAD XIII to score ten victories. Marked with a red '15', edged white and with the blue, red and yellow comet Squadron insignia, it also carried the name Meyer III beneath the cockpit. Ten black iron crosses around the blue comet circle denoted his kills.

31
SPAD XIII S4489 flown by Capt C J Biddle, 13th Aero Squadron, 1918
Having previously flown with SPA.73 and 103rd Aero Squadron, Charles Biddle claimed five of his seven victories commanding the 13th. This Kellner-built SPAD was assigned to the 13th on 7 July 1918. The Squadron's insignia was a white running skeletal grim reaper, complete with scythe. The scythe handle was brown while the sharp end was blood red! Captain Biddle's personal livery included a blue and white radiator cowl and a commander's tricolour band. Note the five victory notches in the scythe and four crosses behind the skeleton (probably denoting bullet strikes).

32
SPAD XIII S4523 flown by Capt E V Rickenbacker, 94th Aero Squadron, 1918
The famous Uncle Sam's Hat-in-Ring insignia was on all the 94th machines. This camouflaged SPAD XIII was marked with a white '1', edged red. Rick's machines also had blue wheel covers with a white star and red centre circle. There was also a red, white and blue band around the forward undercarriage strut.

33
SPAD XIII S15202 flown by Lt F Luke Jr, 27th Aero Squadron, September 1918
Luke scored an amazing 18 kills between 12 and 29 September 1918 only to be shot and killed by German soldiers after crashing on the wrong side of the lines. His aircraft

had the standard French five-colour camouflage. The fuselage carried the Squadron insignia of an eagle on a red circle and the individual aircraft number '26' in black, edged white. This was one of several SPADs he used.

34
SPAD XIII S7525 flown by Lt Chester Wright, 93rd Aero Squadron, late 1918
Wright's machine was in standard five-colour French camouflage, with the 93rd's Indian-head insignia on the fuselage sides and individual aircraft number '2' in white edged red. The '2' was repeated on the top starboard wing just inboard of the roundel. Chester Wright was the top scorer of the 93rd Aero.

35
SPAD XIII S15034 flown by Lt Hamilton Coolidge, 94th Aero Squadron, late 1918
Coolidge had scored eight victories before being killed in action on 27 October 1918, just two weeks before the war's end. Bleriot-built SPAD XIII has standard French five-colour camouflage with blue engine cowling and the Squadron's Hat-in-Ring insignia. The individual aircraft number '22', yellow with red shadow-shading, aft of the insignia is repeated on the top starboard wing inboard of the roundel. Coolidge flew this aircraft for the last time on 3 October when he shot down a balloon, a Fokker D VII and an LVG two-seater.

36
SPAD XIII S15191 'VIRGINIA-ANN' flown by 1st Lt Karl Schoen, 139th Aero Squadron, 1918
Karl Schoen helped shoot down seven enemy aircraft during September and October 1918 before being shot down and killed in a dogfight on 29 October. Unusually Schoen's 'VIRGINIA-ANN' had a blue-grey background to the Mercury squadron emblem. The white outline to the red numerals has been overpainted in green to reduce its visibility in combat.

BIBLIOGRAPHY

America's First Eagles, Lt Lucien H Thayer, R James Bender Publishing, 1983
Hostile Skies, James J Hudson, Syracuse University Press, 1968
In Clouds of Glory, James J Hudson, University of Arkansas Press, 1990
Over the Front, N Franks and F W Bailey, Grub Street, 1992
Wings of Honor, James J Sloan Jr, Schiffer Publishing Ltd, 1994

INDEX

Figures in **bold** refer to illustrations (commentary locators in brackets)

COMPANION SERIES FROM OSPREY

ESSENTIAL HISTORIES
Concise studies of the motives, methods and repercussions of human conflict, spanning history from ancient times to the present day. Each volume studies one major war or arena of war, providing an indispensable guide to the fighting itself, the people involved, and its lasting impact on the world around it.

CAMPAIGN
Accounts of history's greatest conflicts, detailing the command strategies, tactics, movements and actions of the opposing forces throughout the crucial stages of each campaign. Full-color battle scenes, 3-dimensional 'bird's-eye views', photographs and battle maps guide the reader through each engagement from its origins to its conclusion.

ORDER OF BATTLE
The greatest battles in history, featuring unit-by-unit examinations of the troops and their movements as well as analysis of the commanders' original objectives and actual achievements. Color maps including a large fold-out base map, organizational diagrams and photographs help the reader to trace the course of the fighting in unprecedented detail.

ELITE
This series focuses on uniforms, equipment, insignia and unit histories in the same way as Men-at-Arms but in more extended treatments of larger subjects, also including personalities and techniques of warfare.

NEW VANGUARD
The design, development, operation and history of the machinery of warfare through the ages. Photographs, full-colour artwork and cutaway drawings support detailed examinations of the most significant mechanical innovations in the history of human conflict.

WARRIOR
Insights into the daily lives of history's fighting men and women, past and present, detailing their motivation, training, tactics, weaponry and experiences. Meticulously researched narrative and full-color artwork, photographs, and scenes of battle and daily life provide detailed accounts of the experiences of combatants through the ages.

MEN-AT-ARMS
The uniforms, equipment, insignia, history and organisation of the world's military forces from earliest times to the present day. Authoritative text and full-colour artwork, photographs and diagrams bring over 5000 years of history vividly to life.

COMBAT AIRCRAFT
The world's greatest military aircraft and combat units and their crews, examined in detail. Each exploration of the leading technology, men and machines of aviation history is supported by unit listings and other data, artwork, scale plans, and archival photography.